For over twenty years, **Alexis Zen** has been working in top Fortune 500 companies all around the world, focusing on change, transformation, and process improvements. Having a passion for self-development and a calling to help people achieve what they want has led him to create a powerful step-by-step process that will transform your life forever.

When Alexis discovered how to build a wellness company (Mindbodism), develop an application for it, write a self-help book, become a USA TODAY bestselling author, lose 7 kilos, and launch a basketball platform (Basketble) in just three months while he was working full time in a bank and had to care for his newborn baby, he knew he had discovered a powerful SECRET.

He now shares his knowledge and experience through his life coaching, his books, and the online course "The Power of 1 Second: How to achieve anything you want," so others can also manifest anything they want in their lives.

Alexis holds a bachelor's degree in engineering, a master's in operations management, and an executive master's in business administration (EMBA). He is also a motivational speaker, writer, teacher, and entrepreneur, having created two companies: Basketble Ltd., which helps people find a place to play basketball, and Mindbodism Ltd., which helps people become healthier, happier, and more successful.

He is also a Meditation, Qi Gong, Yoga, Kundalini Awakening, and Latin dance teacher, Life Coach, Level 3 Reiki, and Transcendental Meditation (TM) Practitioner.

He loves helping change people's lives and bringing their dreams to fruition.

You can connect with Alexis at www.AlexisZen.com

Other Books by Alexis Zen

Luminary Leadership
(Co-author)

My Spiritual Reality
(Expected November 2023)

Alexis Zen

USA TODAY BESTSELLING AUTHOR

THE POWER OF 1 SECOND

How to achieve anything you want.

mindbodism

Mindbodism Ltd.

Registered offices: 13 Westbourne Terrace, London, W23UL, England
For more information about Mindbodism, visit mindbodism.com

First published by Mindbodism in 2022
www.mindbodism.com

The book is registered as follows:

ISBN: 978-1-7391329-0-3 (digital)
ISBN: 978-1-7391329-1-0 (paperback)

Printed in the United Kingdom

Mindbodism books are available at special quantity discounts to use as premiums
and sales promotions or for use in corporate training programs.
For more information, please write to hello@mindbodism.com.

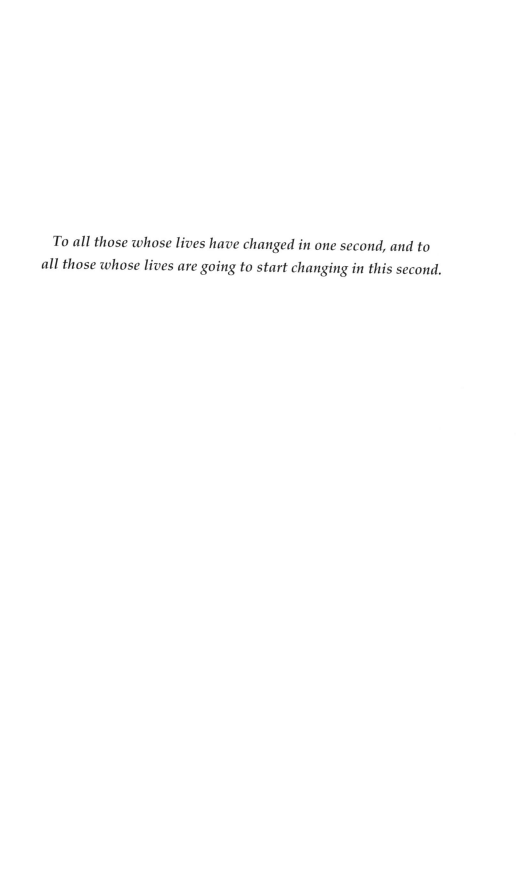

To all those whose lives have changed in one second, and to all those whose lives are going to start changing in this second.

Acknowledgments

The Power of One Second was produced after reviewing hundreds of books and research materials and putting them together in a way that will help people achieve what they want. Therefore, I would like to express gratitude to all the people that have contributed to this book by providing me inspiration, knowledge, and guidance, such as:

Albert Einstein

Napoleon Hill

Eckhart Tolle

Oprah Winfrey

Robin Sharma

Angela Duckworth

Dale Carnegie

Tony Robbins

Stephen R. Covey

Simon Sinek

Charles Duhigg

Aristotle

These people represent but a small fraction of the hundreds of people who have inspired me and provided me with the research materials to be able to write this book.

Also, I am grateful for my wife and son, who give me love every day, and for my parents, who have always been there for me and still help and support me in everything I do.

As a final word of preparation, I offer you this clue to identify the secret power of one second: all achievements have started in one second, and you will know the second it reaches your mind.

Alexis Zen, 2021

Contents

Introduction

Believe it or not, there will be a point in time when your life will change significantly – in just one second. Actually, with every second that passes by, your life is changing by a very small amount; even if you do not do anything, a small change is happening in your life. It can be your relationships, your fitness levels, your financials, your health, your weight, or your experiences, but this change does not help you achieve what you want, does not help you solve your personal or professional problems, and certainly does not bring you closer in making your dreams come true.

Now, imagine that instead of doing nothing or doing something based on your moods, you use the power of one second to direct your energy and actions into something you want to achieve. Now, every second has a purpose, and every second has power, and with this power, you can take control and transform your life. You can become the person you always wanted to be, and you can achieve anything that you want, a lot faster.

Having used the power of one second and the formula of achievement described in this book, I was able to significantly transform my life in just three months:

- I was even able to finish writing the book, which I had started four years ago and for which I had only written a page.
- I was able to lose seven kilograms and increase my fitness levels.
- I was able to increase my finances by obtaining a new property.
- I was able to improve my relationships with my friends and family.
- I was able to launch my new website (www.basketble.com), a business that helps people find a place to play basketball all over the world, and which I had been trying to launch for four years.

- I was able to create a new company (www.Mindbodism.com), which helps people become healthier, happier, and more successful.

- I was able to enhance my creativity and imagination, and I was able to take complete control of my life.

Now, this is a lot of change happening in only three months, and the trigger was the realization of the power of one second and how I could use it to have a positive and lasting impact on my life.

The power of one second is one of the most potent tools you can use to change your life, but it is also one of the most dangerous. Depending on how you use it, it can have a positive or negative impact on things. It is like fire; you can use fire to burn or to keep you warm.

The aim of this book is to share with you the power of one second and the formula of achievement to help you transform your life and achieve anything you want. By mastering the concepts of this book and putting them into an action plan, you will be able to maximize your performance in all aspects of your life.

The *Power of One Second* has five parts:

Part 1 explains the power of one second and the formula of achievement that you can use to transform your life.

Part 2 illustrates how to achieve anything you want by teaching you the process of achievement and how you can condition your mind, create energy, and maintain momentum to start transforming your life – don't stop until you achieve what you want.

Part 3 shows you how to achieve what you want without making sacrifices. It explains how you can change your view of the world, create a plan, create time, maximize your resources, train your brain, use the two superpowers you already have, and predict the future, so you do not have to sacrifice your life to achieve your goals.

Part 4 explains how to find the path you need to follow by finding your life purpose, following your logic and intuition, reflecting on your path, and linking your path to happiness, so you can see that there are many ways to achieve what you want.

Finally, Part 5 illustrates how to follow your path in the *right* way, explaining why you need to follow your own goal, have balance in your life, focus on love, and have moral excellence.

The book is based on the system theory, in which the system is <u>you</u>. By changing certain parts of the system and making them work together, you will be able to achieve more than with its individual parts. Once we explain how the system works and which factors influence it, you will be able to use the actions and tools in this book to transform your life today.

In order to understand how the system works, think of the circle of nature. For instance, flowers grow, die, and grow again. Have you ever found yourself going in a circle? Do you start something, stop, and then again, never achieve what you want because you can never finish?

You start going to the gym, but then you do not find the motivation, so you stop going. You start building a business, but then you do not have the energy to continue, so you stop. And no matter what you do, you are always stuck in this circle.

The good news is that due to how the system is constructed, it is only a matter of time before your state will change again, and you will start doing the things you want to achieve. However, this can take a long time. If you use the power of one second and the formula of achievement, however, not only will you be able to start changing your life *today*, but you will also follow through until you achieve your goals.

Most self-help books offer advice about how to do things, and for many books, you need to be in the right state of mind to benefit from them. They also usually want you to sacrifice in order to achieve what you want. Not this book – the power of one second and the formula of achievement are so strong that it can work independently from your state, and you do not have to sacrifice anything to achieve what you want. That is why it is so powerful.

To start experiencing the power of one second, just straighten your back, think of something funny that made you laugh in the past, and then give a big smile to yourself. If you pay close attention to your mood, you will realize that it has changed, and you have started feeling a bit more positive – laughter triggers healthy physical and emotional changes in your body. It only takes one second to change your mood, and it only takes one second to change your life.

Let's take this second to change your life.

PART 1:

THE POWER OF ONE SECOND AND
THE FORMULA OF ACHIEVEMENT

1.
The Power of One Second

The Power of One Second is a rule and not a law. A law is rigid, and once enacted, everyone must follow it; a rule is a guideline, provided to help people who choose to follow it. It is your choice if you want to follow, it when you want to follow it, and if you even believe in it. It is a kickstart, a way of doing things faster, easier and making the impossible things for you possible.

The basis of the Power of One Second is that **all the change that happens around you or within you happens in one second.**

Just stop for one second and think of an event, a decision, or even a thought that within one second your life, changed your emotions or your actions. Maybe it made you happy or depressed. It could be a wedding proposal, meeting a new person and falling in love at first sight, or someone saying I love you. It could have even happened the death of someone close. In all these cases, the "one-second" impacted your life.

It is the same with your decisions. Think of the one-second decision you may have made to buy, sell, or start a company, which led you to increase or decrease your wealth. The one-second decision you took to go to university had an impact on your relationships, such as finding a best friend, a future business partner, or even a wife or husband. Or the one-second decision you took to apply for a new job that impacted your health, well-being, finances, and relationships.

It is also the same with your thoughts. In one second, you might have had a thought that made you try something new, like visiting a different country or learning to dance. By reading a book or listening to someone, thoughts could be generated in one second to change your mood, change the way you behave and act, or even change your life.

I am sure by now you have found a few examples of your life being changed in one second. You are not the only person.

Archimedes was a Greek mathematician, physicist, and engineer, who, in one second, discovered the Archimedes principle, just by entering his bath and watching the water being displaced. He determined that by measuring the water displacement, you could measure the volume of the immersed objects. He ran naked through the streets, screaming "Eureka!" – which means "I found it" in Greek – completely forgetting, in his excitement, to wear any clothes.

Another example is Sir Isaac Newton, who discovered the law of gravity, in one second, when an apple fell on his head. He realized that the apple always fell perpendicularly, which led him to uncover the law of gravity.

Similarly, Alexander Fleming discovered penicillin, one of the most critical antibiotics, in one second, after returning home and observing that mold had prevented the natural growth of staphylococcus, a bacterium he was studying.

Now, analyzing these examples, we can all see that it took these people one second to change their lives and the lives of others. However, there is one more important similarity in all these examples: these individuals all **paid attention and became aware, just for one second.** It was not the first time Archimedes took a bath, Sir Isaac Newton saw fruit falling from trees, or Alexander Fleming looked at the mold. However, they all became aware for one second.

The Power of One Second is that you only need a moment – one second – to change your life.

The power of one second also states that you have what you need right now – you just need to pay attention and become aware for one second.

THE POWER OF ONE SECOND · 9

There are many more examples we can notice in our everyday lives if we observe carefully that one second makes a difference. In sports, a one-second difference can take someone from winning or losing. A great example is Michael Jordan, one of the greatest basketball players in history. In one second, the Cleveland Cavaliers were eliminated from the 1989 post-season when he scored in the last second, giving the Bulls a 101-100 victory against the Cavaliers. NBA history has more than 700 examples of games that were won in the last second.

It is also applicable to your desires. It takes one second to realize that you are thirsty and want to drink water; it takes one second to realize you are hungry and want to eat; it takes one second to feel you are in love with a person and you cannot live without them.

Obviously, there is a build-up of events, actions, and interactions before the one-second changes everything around you and within you, but there is a way – using the Power of One Second – to make the change now, make the change last, and achieve everything you want in one second. You just need to become aware of the Power of One Second and follow the Formula of Achievement.

However, many people have used the Power of One Second to start their journey without realizing it, but they still face problems – there are so many distractions, choices, influences, and even misfortunes. Even when you start something, you are not always able to finish it; you postpone it, you delay it, and then, in the end, you quit. Have you also experienced that?

Please do not stress yourself because you are not alone. We have all been there. We have all experienced great motivation that initiated action but then stopped. I started writing this book four years ago, and I had only written one page for three and a half years. I started Basketble.com, and for four years, I was not able to create an online platform – until I used the formula of this book. The reason this happened is that, after some time, motivation can die, and then action stops. This is normal, however.

So do not be harsh on yourself. It is easier to have the disorder than order, it is easier not to try rather than win, and it is easier to eat that piece of chocolate than resist the temptation.

The first thing you need to realize is that it is normal behaviour because the brain tends to prefer to do things that are easy rather than difficult.

However, by thinking with the Power of One Second, you will realize that you can continue, even if it is for only one extra second. But that second can make all the difference – it can be an extra push-up while exercising that could make your muscles grow or an extra second of studying a topic that can give you the inspiration to start or do something new. It can be an extra second of energy that provides a runner with the boost he needs to finish the race. It can be that extra inch, as described by Al Pacino in his famous speech in the movie *Any Given Sunday*: "That's gonna make the f*king difference between losing and winning, between living and dying."

**When you are about to stop,
believe you can continue for one second.**

Once you do that, your momentum will continue. It is like when you push a ball on the floor: at first, there is resistance, and friction, because there is no energy. Then there is momentum, and the ball is rolling. Then there is more friction and resistance, which tries to stop the ball. This friction is your inner voice, which will try to stop you, to convince you to take the easy path. You must believe you can continue for one more second and build more momentum: do not let the motivation die.

Socrates, the famous Greek philosopher, created the analogy that Athens was like a sluggish horse that needed a fly to bite it, so the horse could be awakened to continue its course. That fly was Socrates, and your fly is the one second you need to use every time you feel you are moving away from your goal or realize that you have stopped trying. It only takes one second to bring you back on track.

**When you have moved away from your course,
think you can come back in one second.**

However, time is fixed, and tasks are piling up. You have so many things to do and no time at all. "What do I do?" you ask. Think again. Are you spending all your time on the important things that will improve your life? Are you using every second to complete an action that will help you achieve what you want? Think again.

**A day has 86,400 seconds,
and every second counts – use them wisely.**

When you realize you have thousands of seconds available to you each day and realize you must make every single second count, then you will think differently and stop giving excuses – such as "I do not have time" – because you have thousands of seconds to spend. Then, when you value every second you spend, and you do not let any second go wasted, you will also realize that by paying attention to just one second at a time, your life will not be wasted and by using the Power of One Second wisely, you will be able to achieve anything you want.

2.
The Formula for Achievement

By now, you will be starting to see the importance of one second and what impact it can make on someone's life. We know that one second is very important, and by looking in the past, I am sure you have already found examples of seconds in your life that changed things. Personally, many of the important things in my life – on professional, personal, and even spiritual levels – happened in one second.

I built my first business, Basketble.com, in one second. It was a cold, rainy evening, and I was in my small rented studio flat in London, just off Regent Street. I had been living there for six months, and even though I loved playing basketball, I could not find anywhere to play. I could not play outside because most of the time it was either too cold or it was raining, and I could not play indoors because I did not have any friends and the courts were very expensive to book. I could not even play in other people's basketball sessions because they were all fully booked. So, I would sit in front of my computer, watching the raindrops race each other down my windowpane, and remember when I used to live in Greece and play basketball outdoors every day.

Times back then were different; every day after school, I would go home, study quickly, run to the outdoor basketball court, near my house, and play basketball. It was fun because I would meet other players, and then we would all play together for hours until it was too dark to see the basketball – the courts back then did not have any lights.

But there was nowhere to play basketball in London – at least until that second that I called a basketball court near Kings Cross and asked to book my own court. Then everything changed; people seeing me playing basketball by myself, asked if they could join me. Then more people learned about the session and would come. When the session became too crowded, I hired another court, as I did not want anyone to experience the disappointment of not finding a place to play basketball. When people wanted to play more competitively, I started a basketball league.

And then, very recently, in just one second, I realized that I decided to launch my company's website, which helps promote everyone's basketball sessions around the world, so that one day you can play basketball anywhere, anytime.

At difficult times, remember that life will always give you what you need, not necessarily what you want.

If I had not experienced the difficulty and disappointment of struggling to find a place to play basketball, then I might not have created the Basketble.com business, and not have helped thousands of people.

On a personal level, my life has also changed in one second, in particular the second I met my wife. It was the summer of 2013, and I was on holiday with two friends of mine, Serginio, and Grigorious. We were on the Greek island of Mykonos, a place I am sure most of you know about, as it is one of the most cosmopolitan islands in the world. It is a great place because it combines amazing food, beautiful beaches, great entertainment, and traditional white houses.

Back then, it was completely different and more authentic, but still, a place to meet new people. So, as a single guy, what better place to go on holiday than Mykonos? After staying there for a week, Serginios asked me to go with him to the island of Koufonisia.

Koufonisia is a small island around one and a half hours from Mykonos, and completely different – there are no cars and only one main small bar. Very few tourists visited the island, and when I tried to think of a reason

THE FORMULA FOR ACHIEVEMENT · 15

to do so, I could not. However, one hour before Serginios left, I decided to go with him – in one second, of course.

There was a full moon that night, and when we arrived, Serginios, Grigorious, and I went to the bar, Soroko, located near the sea. It was a magical place: large pillows on the floor next to the ocean, lounge music, great cocktails, and moonlight reflecting on the dark water. And just five meters away, a very beautiful young woman, drinking gin with her aunt. I was doing the same with my friends. When I saw that a guy sitting next to Natalia, my future wife, was leaving, I decided – suddenly, in one second, and without thinking – to sit down next to her.

I had no idea why I was doing that; I had not planned anything to say to her. Some guys might be scared just to sit next to a woman and start talking. Doing that while the woman drinks with her aunt might sound creepy. And then you might question why this woman even spoke to me after my opening line of "Are you drinking water?" In that second, however, a great love story started, and now we are married and have a beautiful son and daughter together. If it was not for the one second I sat next to her, we might not be together.

Be aware of the Power of One Second and how your life can transform in just a moment.

Finally, my life has changed in one second at the spiritual level. It was February 2020 in London, and I was in a bar near the Thames River, having drinks with some friends. Just before the end of the night, I went outside to get some fresh air. Suddenly, I felt an electric current move from the lower part of my body to my head, forcing me to straighten my body, open my chest, and feel a connection with the universe. In that second, my awareness, my emotions, and my consciousness were completely changed. It felt like I was baptized again, leaving my old self behind.

That one-second experience led me to start a new business, www.mindbodism.com, to help people become happier, healthier, and more successful by using neuroscience, Chinese and Indian practices, and self-development. My next book, *My Spiritual Reality*, explains more about spirituality, my journey, and mindbodism.

**Mindbodism is a new way of living your life,
allowing you to become healthier, happier, and more successful.**

All these one-second changes in my life made me think that instead of waiting for some second in the future to change my life, why wait? Now I can create every second now, every day, so I do not have to wait for the future and change my life now. That took me on a journey to combine my 20-year experience of change, productivity, process improvements, portfolio management, and entrepreneurship with the experience of all great authors on self-improvement, studying hundreds of self-help books and journals on neuroscience and spirituality, all to understand how we operate and how we can achieve what we want.

After all of my research, I have concluded that many concepts and methods in the self-help books were similar. The knowledge is public, so there is a pattern to what all the authors say, but I realized I learned something new from each book.

Each book helped me change in one second how I think and act and helped me become better in all aspects of my life. So never stop reading.

The Formula for Achievement is also influenced by my background and based on a systematic approach – if you follow it, it will work. It is just like a bicycle, waiting for you to take the ride. It is an end-to-end approach, as I am trying to help you by not only showing you how you can achieve what you want but also how to achieve it in the right way and without making sacrifices. There are seven pillars in total:

The 7 Pillars

1. Learn the foundation. The foundation describes the five-step process to achieve what you want. You need to have a goal, so you understand what you want. You need to have a purpose, so you know why you want what you want; a daily ritual, so you can act toward achieving your goal daily; and you need to know the 1+1=2 to understand which actions impact your goal.

Finally, you need to have a feedback loop, so you know if what you are doing moves you closer to your goal or not and if you need to change your actions accordingly.

2. Condition your mind. Once you have the foundation and know the process, you need to work on your mind. You need to believe in what you are doing to achieve it. You need to master your inner voice, so you will not be distracted and stay focused on what you want to achieve. You need to be persistent. Finally, you need to be conscious, to achieve things faster.

3. Create energy. You need to create energy to start acting towards your goal. Thoughts, music, intense emotions, learning, sharing the action with someone, exercising, qi gong and connecting with nature can all help you create energy.

4. Maintain momentum. Using energy can be exhausting, and you might want to stop or quit. Therefore, there is a way to maintain momentum by restoring energy, acting without thinking, focusing on your why, measuring progress, and talking to your believers.

5. Achieve without making sacrifices. There are many ways you can achieve what you want without sacrificing. You can change your view of the world, create a plan, create time, maximize your resources, train your brain, use your two superpowers, and predict the future.

6. Find the path you need to follow. You can take many paths, but you need to understand the differences and choose your own way. You can follow a path based on logic or intuition, but you need to reflect on the path you have taken and link your path to happiness.

7. Follow your path in the right way. You can achieve your goal in many ways, but it is better to achieve it in the "right" way. It has to be *your* goal that you are trying to achieve, and you need balance in what you do. You need to focus on love and have moral excellence based on integrity, respect, and philotimo, which means to befriend your honour.

PART 2:

HOW TO ACHIEVE
ANYTHING YOU WANT

3.
Learn the Foundation

In this chapter, we will explore the five steps to achieving what you want.

STEP 1: THE GOAL

"Ask, and you will receive."
Luke 11:9

This book will help you achieve what you want, but the most critical question you need to ask yourself is: *What do I actually want?*

It is essential to answer this question because it will create purpose in your life. It does not have to be your life purpose; it can be something simple, like waking up in the morning, beginning to exercise, or changing your mood. Knowing what it is that you want is a significant first step in achieving your goal.

You can only answer this question, and the better you know yourself, the more confident you will be about what you want – and the easier it will be to achieve it.

So, what do you want to achieve? If the answer is not clear to you yet, you can try answering the following questions:

1. Do you want to do something that you are passionate about? (Write a book, play your favourite sport)

2. Do you have an unexplained drive or calling for something that you want to pursue? (Help people, start your own business)

3. Is there anything you have wanted to do in the past or want to do but keep postponing? (Go to the gym, start eating healthy food, read a book)

4. Did you begin to do something in the past and stop, but now you want to start again? (Exercise, focus on your self-development)

5. Is there something you want to do before you leave this earth? (Buy your dream car or house, meet the love of your life)

By writing what you want, you are programming your mind to think about the thing you want to do, and as you are reading this book, you are programming your mind to create associations between the things you have read in the book and what you want. When you have a goal, your frontal lobe will scan the whole brain to find a way to achieve your goal, engaging different networks of neurons related to your goal based on your current knowledge and experience. (This is why most successful people read a lot – it creates new connections in the brain, so next time there is a problem, there will be a bigger database to help.) Also, by having a goal, you can be more productive and driven, as you will find a reason for waking up in the morning and wanting to reach your goal.

When defining your goal, you need to be specific so that you can measure it and set a time frame. You cannot improve what you cannot measure. Additionally, the time frame will affect your plan and approach. You would need different plans to earn 10,000 pounds within a year and 100,000 pounds within a year.

It is also okay to set unrealistic goals because the process of doing so will enhance your creativity and imagination. However, this can only work if you have the right mindset: you need to see failure as success and know that every failure brings you a step closer to your goal. If you do not have this mindset, setting unrealistic goals can work against you and prevent you from reaching your real purpose – your inner voice will tell you to quit out of fear of failure.

Let's see some examples of setting a specific and measurable goal:

Instead of saying, "I want to lose weight," say, "I want to lose two kilograms in one month," and then set the exact date.

Instead of saying, "I want to be more fit," say, "I want to start to train 30 minutes each day."

Instead of saying, "I want to be a millionaire," say, "In two years, I want to have one million pounds in my bank account," and set the date.

Think: *What measurable result do I want and by when?* Complete the following.

I want to...   **(by   )**

Some of you might feel that you do not want to write down your goal because you think you cannot achieve it. Stop doing that – the only thing you need to do at this point is present and think about what you want to achieve. Use the Power of One Second and start writing your goal now. It can be small or big, but you must write it down now.

I know that many of you are excited and probably want to write more than one goal, but you should resist the temptation unless you already know how to work with multiple goals. Once you master one goal, you can replicate the system and add more goals using the following categories.

1. Self-development (skills you want to develop: learn piano, study books, etc.)

2. Health/Fitness (diet, exercise, weight, etc.)

3. Relationships (family, friends, networking, etc.)

4. Financial/Business (income, investments, businesses, etc.)

5. Material (things you want to buy: a car, clothes, a house etc.)

See some examples below:

Self-Development

> **Goal 1:** I want to get a Level 1 piano certification by the 23rd of November 2021.

Health/Fitness

> **Goal 1:** I want to lose two kilograms by the 1st of July.

Relationships

> **Goal 1:** I want to improve my relationship with my family daily.

Financial/Business

> **Goal 1:** I want to build my own business by the 10th of December 2021.

Material

> **Goal 1:** I want to buy a car by the 1st of December 2021.

Now that you have written down your goal, you will need to create the following affirmation and read it aloud when you wake up and before you go to sleep. Affirmations can boost confidence, reduce fear and anxiety, and help you start visualizing the person you want to become, bringing you closer to what you want to achieve.

Before you start your affirmation, stand or sit in a comfortable posture, close your eyes, and raise your arms on the side until they reach above your head. Slowly breathe in and connect your palms, holding your breath for one second and then exhaling slowly, bringing your connected palms towards your chest.

You will become more focused on what you are saying, and you will connect with yourself, so the affirmation becomes more powerful.

By <date> I will <goal>. I know I can achieve this goal because I will <action> daily, and I will not stop until I <goal>. I believe that I can <goal>, and I know I can overcome every difficulty I find in my way because I have faith. I can <write what you will see, feel, hear, smell, or taste when you have achieved your goal, in detail, trying to use all of your five senses and connect your goal to something higher than you>.

See the example below:

By 30 of November 2021, I will finish writing *The Power of One Second*. I know I can achieve this goal because I will write quality material daily, and I will not stop until I finish writing this book. I believe that I can write this book, and I know I can overcome any difficulty I find in my way because I have faith. I can see the cover of my book is published on Amazon, and I can feel the excitement of achieving my goal. I can hear people talking about my book and attending seminars to see how I can help them to change their lives and achieve anything they want. I can even smell the book, which has just been printed, which reminds me of the books I used to buy at school.

It is a very powerful affirmation that you should not underestimate. It contains a few words that can help you along your journey, including **belief.** When you believe you can achieve something, you will achieve it because it boosts your confidence, and, as we explained, the brain will start making new connections to help, you achieve your goal. Together with the daily activities, you will become unstoppable.

The other word is **faith.** Faith is such a powerful word, which is also used many times in the Bible, such as Jesus Christ saying, ' Faith has made you well" or "Faith has saved you." When you have faith, you do not need to think or find a reason for your success, and that is very powerful. When you are depressed, bankrupt, or ill – no matter what misfortune has occurred in your life – but you have faith, it is only a matter of time until you will find a way to overcome your difficulties, solve your problems, and achieve what you want.

STEP 2: **THE PURPOSE**

"He who has a why can endure anyhow."
Friedrich Nietzsche

You have now defined your what, but you will also have to ask **why** you want what you want.

You need to know why because we are more likely to accept change when we know the reason for the change. Subconsciously you can be more accepting of change, and your why will also act as a motivating factor.

Suppose you want to stop smoking. If you have not found a reason why to quit, you will most likely not quit. On the contrary, if you have a strong reason – like you were going to die – you would most likely quit smoking immediately. The closer your "why" is to your heart, the stronger the impact you will feel, and the stronger the motivation will be to achieve your goal.

Also, knowing your why will help you prioritize if you have multiple goals. For example, if you want to buy a car but also go on an expensive trip around the world, knowing your why can determine which goal you want to achieve first.

See some examples below:

Self-Development

Goal 1: I want to get a Level 1 piano certification by the 23rd of November 2021.

Why: Because I feel inspired when I play the piano.

Health/Fitness

Goal 1: I want to lose two kilograms by the 1st of July.

Why: Because I want to look leaner.

Relationships

Goal 1: I want to improve my relationship with my family daily.

Why: Because I love them, and do not want to disappoint them.

Financial/Business

Goal 1: I want to build my own business by the 10th of December 2021.

Why: Because I want to generate a second stream of income.

Material

Goal 1: I want to buy a car by the 1st of December 2021.

Why: Because I want to drive around, instead of using the public transport

Think, *Why do I want to achieve this goal?* Then complete your own "whys."

STEP 3: **THE DAILY RITUAL**

**There is no true commitment unless you
are committed to working on your goal daily.**

When you commit to working on your goal daily, a huge mindset shift happens. One of the main reasons you are failing to achieve what you want might be because you fail to work on your goal daily. The daily ritual is **daily action** towards achieving your goal.

Your goal is the food you give to your body; if you do not nourish yourself daily, then the body cannot function to its full potential. Working on your goal and completing activities daily and throughout the day has many benefits. Let's explore a few by using the following example:

Suppose your goal is to read a book in a week, and you have planned to start and finish reading the book on Sunday.

First of all, if something happens on Sunday, and you cannot spend any time reading the book, or you do not have as much time as anticipated to finish reading the book, this means you will fail to reach your goal.

On the other hand, if you set aside 30 minutes each day, even if something happens on Sunday, it will be easier to find 30 minutes to complete your goal.

Secondly, by repeating this activity daily, you will create a habit, that will not happen if you only do it once a week. Creating a habit will save you energy – you will no longer have to overthink about reading the book since this decision will be automated. Also, if you do not read one day, you will feel that something is missing, and you will be inclined to start reading a book. Choose a time of day with no disruptions and try to work on your goal at that same time each day. First thing in the morning, before you start working, is one of the best; also, as you will be completing a part of the goal daily, you will feel happier, which releases dopamine.

Finally, by practicing every day, you will get the benefits of the activity more quickly, as you will not have to wait until the end of the week to realize and experience the benefit of this activity. Also, the activity will be easier to perform and focus on, as you will spend less time on it each day. For example:

Self-Development

Goal 1: I want to get a Level 1 piano certification by the 23rd of November 2021.

Why: Because I feel inspired when I play the piano.

Daily Ritual: I will dedicate one hour each day at 8:00 A.M. to practice playing the piano

Health/Fitness

Goal 1: I want to lose two kilograms by 01st of July.

Why: Because I want to look leaner.

Daily Ritual: I will dedicate 60 minutes each day at 7:00 A.M. to exercise.

Relationships

Goal 1: I want to improve my relationship with my family daily.

Why: Because I love them, and do not want to disappoint them.

Daily Ritual: I will dedicate three hours each day at 7:00 P.M. to read about improving my relationships with family and spending time with them.

Financial/Business

Goal 1: I want to build my own business by (10th of December 2021)

Why: Because I want to generate a second stream of income.

Daily Ritual: I will dedicate two hours each day at 5:00 P.M. to create a plan to start my own business.

Material

Goal 1: I want to buy a car by 01st of December 2021.

Why: Because I want to drive around, instead of using public transport.

Daily Ritual: I will dedicate 10 minutes each day at 10:00 P.M. to plan how I will manage to buy a car.

Think, *how much time will I dedicate daily to achieve my goal?* The more time you commit, the faster you will reach your goal.

Goal 1:

Why: Because…

Daily ritual: I will dedicate (hours) each day at (PM/AM) to (the action you will).

If you have multiple goals, indicate the hours per day you will spend completing your goal, and the daily actions you will take towards attaining your goal. The fewer goals you have, the more focused you will be, and the faster you will reach that particular goal. To simplify things, if one goal takes three hours of effort and your available time per day is three hours, if you just spend all of your available time on that goal, you will finish it in one day. On the other hand, if you spend only one hour per day on that goal and do something else for the remaining two available hours, you will finish that goal in three days instead.

Remember that the time you spend each day on these goals might change in the future, as you will need to evaluate whether the hours you spend on your goal will allow you to meet your target date. Also, based on your lifestyle, some days, you might want to spend more time on one goal and less time on another. The most important thing, however, is to work on all your goals daily – though you can be free to adjust the duration and intensity of the goal, depending on your needs and progress.

For example, if your goal is to exercise for 30 minutes daily, maybe one day you can exercise for ten minutes and then stretch instead of doing an intense workout.

The secret is to work on your goals daily, to create the habit. The daily ritual has a secret power: the only thing that matters is what you do now, so where you spend every second will determine when you can achieve your goal.

STEP 4: 1+1=2: THE ACTIONS IMPACTING YOUR GOAL

"I have not failed. I have found 10,000 ways that won't work."
Thomas Edison

Every action you take impacts your goal to some degree, but no goal can be achieved if there is no action. Also, even the actions that have no effect on your goal might help you indirectly attain your goals, either by helping you create a new idea or by directing your focus on other actions that might impact your goals.

It is the reason I have created the simple concept of 1+1= 2.

1+ 1 = 2 (Action 1 + Action 2 = Attainment of Goal)

The important thing to understand is that there is always a relationship between your actions and the attainment of your goal. Remember that if number two is your goal, then the numbers on the left-hand side of the equation represent not only your actions but the impact that these actions will have on your goal. Your actions can lead you to positive or negative results, or even no result if that action has no relationship to your goal. However, what is worth remembering is that if you stop taking any action, you will not be able to achieve your goal, and even the actions that do not directly impact your goal will always help you.

For example, John wants to earn $100,000 in one year. He can find two jobs each giving him $50,000 per year after tax ($50,000 + $50,000= $100,000), or he can earn the $100,000 by finding four jobs that pay $25,000 each ($25,000 + $25,000 + $25,000 + $25,000= $100,000). In the latter, he will need to complete more actions to earn $100,000 per year since each job is giving him $25,000. Also, as we discussed, not all of your actions can have a positive impact on your goal – but the good news is, as long as you do not stop, and as long as you take another action to compensate for the negative impact, you can still achieve your goal.

And remember what we said before:

Life will give you what you need, not what you want, so have faith and continue your actions. Believe, and you will succeed.

Using the previous example, suppose John lost one of his jobs and now earns $75,000. As long as he does not give up, has faith, and believes he can find a new job, he will find a new job that offers him $25,000 or more, allowing him to achieve his goal. If he finds a job for less, he will need to either increase his earnings from the existing jobs or find an extra job. The important thing for him to remember is that nothing can stop him; if he has faith and continues his actions, it will only be a matter of time before he achieves anything he wants.

As I have said, even an action that does not impact your goal can indirectly help you achieve it. So, if John set up his own business, and it did not produce any revenue, which did not allow him to achieve the desired $100,000 earnings, his actions still will not go to waste. Someday, what he has learned from the experience will help him generate additional revenue. An example of this is Dan Lok, who failed in 13 business ventures over three years before ultimately becoming a multimillionaire.

Your goals and your actions need to be measurable and time-specific. Otherwise, you will be unable to monitor progress, and it will be more challenging to see what you need to do to achieve your goal. Let's now look at an example:

Julia had a goal to lose two kilograms in one month, and, using the 1+1=2 Rule, she identified the relationship between her goals and her actions. By exercising and reducing the amount of food she eats, she will be able to achieve her goal of losing two kg in one month.

So, start exercise + reduce the amount of food = lose two kilograms in one month.

After one month, she measured herself and saw she had lost only one kilogram. Now, since she did not measure her actions, she cannot know what to change and by how much.

However, if she had been more specific in setting her actions, and written her formula like the one below, she would be able to know what to change.

Eat 2,000 calories daily + exercise ten minutes every day = lose two kilograms in one month.

Now, if after one month she lost only one kilogram, she will know what her baseline (i.e., 2,000 calories and 10 minutes every day) was, and she will know that it is not enough, so she will have to adjust her calorie intake and/or the time she spends exercising. This is why not only the goals but the actions need to be measured and be time-specific.

This also works for more abstract goals. For example, if your goal is to reduce stress, try to make your goal measurable, so you can see if your actions made a difference. Instead of setting the goal as "reduce stress," define your goal as "achieve ten days without stress."

Remember your actions need to be measurable and time-specific and need to have a direct impact on your goal. The more knowledge you have about the goal and what effects it has, the easier it will be to identify the actions that have the most significant impact. If you do not know the actions that impact your goal, then start with one action in particular: **I will spend x number of hours a day researching which actions would impact my goal** or use the shortcut of hiring someone who has already achieved the same goal.

Below you can find some specific actions that relate to the goals:

Self-Development

Goal 1: I want to get a Level 1 piano certification by the 3rd of November 2021.

Why: Because I feel inspired when I play the piano.

Daily ritual: I will dedicate one hour each day at 8:00 A.M. to practice playing the piano.

- **Action 1:** Practice playing the piano daily (60 minutes).

Health/Fitness

Goal 1: I want to lose two kilograms by the 01ˢᵗ of July.

Why: Because I want to look leaner.

Daily ritual: I will dedicate 60 minutes each day at 7:00 A.M. to exercise.

- **Action 1:** Run daily (30 minutes).

- **Action 2:** Do cardio exercises daily (30 minutes).

Relationships

Goal 1: I want to improve my relationship with my family, daily.

Why: Because I love them, and do not want to disappoint them.

Daily ritual: I will dedicate three hours each day at 7:00 P.M. to reading about improving my relationships with family and spending time with them.

- **Action 1:** Study how to improve relationships daily (30 minutes).

- **Action 2:** Spend time with my family daily (2.5 hours).

Financial/Business

Goal 1: I want to build my own business by the 10ᵗʰ of December 2021.

Why: Because I want to generate a second stream of income.

Daily ritual: I will dedicate two hours each day at 5:00 P.M. to create a plan to start my own business.

- **Action 1:** Research how to build a business and create a plan (2 hours).

Material

Goal 1: I want to buy a car by the 01ˢᵗ of December 2021.

Why: Because I want to drive around, instead of using public transport.

Daily ritual: I will dedicate ten minutes each day at 10:00 P.M. to plan how I will manage to buy a car.

- **Action 1:** Identify the car I want to buy, and determine how to finance it (10 minutes).

The critical thing to remember is to stay focused on the time you spend achieving your goal and assess if your actions are helping you to do so. You will often find that some of the actions have been completed, so you will have to remove them. Other actions may need to be changed completely, or you may need to increase the time you spend on them, to help you achieve your goal in your desired timeframe.

So, next time you start complaining that you cannot achieve what you want, then try to answer the following two questions:

1. What are you doing about it?
2. Which actions do you need to complete, and what needs to change to help you reach your goal?

Again, do not be afraid, and do not worry if you do not believe you can achieve it at the moment. You just need to follow the process. In the next chapter, I will show you how to strengthen your beliefs, overcome your fears, and create energy, so you can start acting on your goals. And do not forget to use your two powerful words: BELIEVE and have FAITH.

There will be a time when you will not be able to work on your goal due to unforeseen situations. Remember the Power of One Second and complete your affirmations if that happens. This will ensure your mind is wired daily to meet your goal, even if it is only for a brief second. You just need to plant the seed, and the growth will come.

Now, using the following template, complete the section for your goal.

Goal Type (Self-Development, Health/Fitness, Relationships, Financial/Business, Material)

Goal 1: I want to _____ by _____.

Why: _____ (Because…)

Daily ritual: I will dedicate _____ hours each day at (A.M./P.M.) to achieve my (specify goal).

- **Action 1:** _____ (time allotted)

- **Action 2:** _____ (time allotted)

STEP 5: THE FEEDBACK LOOP

"Insanity: doing the same thing over and over again and expecting different results."
Albert Einstein

The last step of the foundation is the feedback loop. This is a process in which you analyze the actions impacting your goals, and change or make improvements to your actions to maximize their impact on your goal. This step is crucial because as you get feedback on what works and what does not, you can improve things and reach your goal much more quickly.

If you fail to do this step, you will fail. If we monitor our goals and see something is not working or not impacting our goal, then we need to do something different until we can see an impact on our goal.

For example, suppose George wants to buy a house and needs to save $1,000 monthly for a deposit. If he realizes that he has not saved that much money at the end of the month, he will need to assess what put him off track from his monthly saving target and then reduce that next month. He will have to reduce it even further, so he can compensate for the money he did not save in the first month.

He has taken action – saving money – and his feedback was that he did not save enough money. The change in his action will need to save more money next month. He will need to do the same to ensure he reaches his targets and goals.

However, you must always consider that some actions require some time to materialize. Be cautious, therefore, and disciplined and patient, and increase your knowledge so you know what actions impact your goal and how long it takes to impact your goal. That is why the concept of 1+1 =2 is essential, as discussed in Step 4.

For example, if you are exercising daily because you want to build muscle, it does not mean that your muscle will grow on your second day of doing so. This also does not mean that you are doing something wrong because even if you exercise daily, it takes time to build muscle. If you have the knowledge, and you know that building a muscle requires ten days, then using your feedback loop, do an assessment at ten days to see if you have reached your desired outcome. If you haven't, then it's time to make changes. You can increase intensity or change the type of exercise, and then after ten days, you should monitor your progress again and continue with this loop. Alternatively, you can save ten days by asking an expert to help you, instead of trying by yourself.

Also, using the feedback loop, you can reflect on your progress and determine what is blocking your progress and what you need to do to get back on track. For example, if your goal is to publish a book and you cannot find the time to write it, review where you spend your time and see if you can change your priorities. You can also do things faster, even reduce your sleep or go out a bit less so you can continue taking the actions that will bring you towards your goal.

To Summarise:

The five steps you need to work on to complete the foundation are:

STEP 1: The Goal (What measurable result do you want, and when?)

STEP 2: The Purpose (Why do you want to achieve that goal?)

STEP 3: The Daily Ritual (How much time and what action are you going to dedicate and complete daily to reach your goal and at what time?)

STEP 4: 1+1=2, The Actions Impacting Your Goal (What are you doing about it? Which actions do you need to complete to reach your goal?

STEP 5: The Feedback Loop (Monitor your actions and change them if you see they do not impact your goal, identify anything blocking your progress, and see what you can do to unblock it.)

If you need more support on the foundation, you can send an email at hello@mindbodism.com

4.
Condition Your Mind

You cannot change unless you change something.

You now know what you want and why you want it and have identified actions to help you reach your goal. You have a feedback loop to know what you need to do to improve. However, you still find it difficult to start – what is missing?

STEP 1: ENHANCE YOUR BELIEF

No one should tell you what you can or cannot do, including yourself. The belief you can do does not lie in your inner voice or the voices of others but in your heart.

A belief is to trust that something is true. The magic of the power of belief is that anyone can have it, as it does not depend on proof. For example, people believe in God, even though there is no scientific evidence, and many kids believe in Santa Claus because their parents have told them he exists; they do not need any proof to believe their parents. That is why belief is a magic power, one you can use to help you achieve your goals.

Believe you can do it; you will do it.

There is a great quote from Einstein that said:

"Only those who believe everything is possible
can achieve the things most consider impossible."
Albert Einstein

However, it is easier said than done, as many of us might have a few things in our minds that prevent us from believing or a few fears that do not let us start. First, you should be aware of your main fears and know that once you master your belief and faith, all your fears will disappear. These are some of the main fears:

1. Not having the skills or resources
2. Not knowing what will happen
3. Becoming poor
4. Not succeeding
5. Something terrible will happen
6. Getting hurt or getting sick
7. Someone saying something terrible to us

You should be aware of those fears and see the methods in this chapter to overcome them by enhancing your belief that you can achieve anything you want.

"Fear kills more dreams than failure ever will."

Suzy Kassem

Therefore, if you try, you have a greater chance of success. Fear is human and is real, and the best way to overcome all your fears is to believe you can do it by increasing your self-confidence. The following affirmation practice can help you with this.

You will need to be in a standing position or sitting down with your eyes closed. Raise your hands to your side until you reach your solar plexus line, which is located in your upper abdominal region, just above your belly button. Your palms should face upwards, and you need to make sure that your chest is lifted, to have a straight posture. While you are in this power posture, as you say the affirmation that follows, you should visualize positive energy coming through your palms and charging your solar plexus until you feel confident and powerful.

Repeat the following affirmation any time you have doubts or fears stopping you from believing you can achieve what you want:

I believe I can achieve anything I want. I have faith, so I know it is only a matter of time until I achieve what I want. I believe that with my continuous actions my life will change completely, and I will transform into the person I want to become, and I will be able to achieve anything I want. I believe in my abilities, and I have faith. I can feel the change happening in me; I am confident and powerful and ready to achieve anything I want.

We focus on the solar plexus as we do this affirmation because this is where the third chakra lies. The solar plexus is a source of personal power, warrior energy, and transformation. In Sanskrit the word "chakra" means "wheel" and each chakra represents an energy centre of the body. The more you believe in this affirmation, the more powerful you will become. Some of you may not believe or do not want to believe in chakras, which is okay – however, there is research about how a positive power posture can impact someone's psychology, so believe in that. Just watch Amy's Cuddy TED talk, "Your Body Language Might Shape Who You Are."

Also, you might believe that you can do it, but your belief is not very strong because you think your ultimate goal is too big and unachievable, which relates to your fear of failure. If you have this doubt, make sure you break down your goal into smaller goals.

For example, instead of saying you want to lose 12 kilograms this year, say you want to lose two kilograms this month. When you achieve the first goal, then this can boost your self-confidence and belief. However, if you do not reach your goal, try to focus on your 1+1=2 formula. It is not that you are not capable of achieving your goal; most likely, the actions that you are taking are not impacting your goal, or they might be the right actions but need more time dedicated to them.

Therefore, break down your bigger goals into smaller goals, and think 1+1=2. Find the relationship between your actions and goals, and start doing those that can have an immediate impact. Easy wins can also help you boost your belief because you can see results at an early stage. In business terms, these are also called low-hanging fruit because they are easy and quick to complete. Here are some examples of low-hanging fruit:

Suppose you want to increase the revenue of your business. In that case, it will be easier to start talking to your existing customers and see if they are interested in other products you have, rather than trying to attract new customers.

If you want to write a book, creating a high-level plan with the main topics you want to cover will be easier.

If you want to improve a process, it will be easier to find the existing issues and tackle the issues that are easiest to solve and have the most significant impact.

If you want to start exercising, allocating a few minutes each day will be easier than committing to a two-hour workout.

The method I like to use to identify low-hanging fruit is a combination of brainstorming and the Ishikawa, or fishbone diagram. Brainstorming was invented in 1938 by Alex Osborn, and it is the process in which a group gathers together and shares ideas on how they can potentially solve a problem without criticizing one another. The Ishikawa or fishbone diagram was created by Kaoru Ishikawa in the 1960s, and it shows the potential causes of a specific event. Here you can see how to use the combined method to help identify the low-hanging fruit:

1. Identify what you want to achieve. By doing that, you can reduce the scope of what you are trying to achieve, and you can be more focused.

2. Gather a group of friends, colleagues, or subject matter experts – or you can even do it yourself. By doing this, you will be able to generate ideas to help you achieve your goal. The more people involved, the greater the brainpower, but try not to have more than seven people, otherwise, it will be difficult for everyone to have the opportunity to contribute.

3. Identify what actions will help you achieve your goal. By doing that, you will see that there are many options and actions you can take to achieve your goal.

4. Group the actions by categories. Your brain will generate more actions for each category because it will be even more focused. It will be easier for it to create associations.

5. Choose the actions that are easy to implement, and have the highest impact. By doing that, you will be able to tackle the low-hanging fruit and strengthen your belief that you can achieve because you will see progress.

6. Implement the selected actions. This way, you can complete the actions and get closer to achieving your goal.

For example, if I want to increase the revenue of my basketble.com business, I can do the following:

Step 1: Identify what I want to achieve: My goal is to increase the revenue of my business.

Step 2: I need to determine who will be involved to help me achieve my goal. I can invite my friends or colleagues or hire some experts to do a brainstorming session.

Step 3: Identify the actions that will help grow my revenue, such as these:

- Advertise on Facebook, Instagram
- Advertise on Google Ads
- Give flyers to customers
- Create a promotion
- Hire a salesperson to increase sales
- Create a new basketball session for women

Step 4: Create the categories:

Marketing/Sales

- Advertise on Facebook, Instagram
- Advertise on Google Ads
- Advertise on YouTube
- Give flyers to customers
- Create a promotion
- Hire a salesperson to focus on increasing sales

Customer Support

- Improve the speed of communication with my customers
- Improve the customer experience of attending a basketball session
- Train to cross-sell (suggest similar products to those customers have bought previously)

Product:

- Create a new basketball session for women
- Create a new basketball session for kids
- Create a corporate basketball league

Step 5: Choose the actions with low effort and high impact:

- Train to cross-sell (suggest similar products to those customers have bought previously)
- Advertise on Facebook, Instagram

Note: The low effort/High impact actions are related to the expertise of the individual or the team. For example, if someone has never advertised on Facebook or Instagram, they might not consider it a low-effort action. Therefore, make sure you select the actions for this category based on your available skills.

Step 6: Implement the actions:

By implementing those two actions we saw a significant increase in our revenues. If you think about it if people do not know you exist, how can they buy products from you? Sometimes we are very busy and we cannot see what we are trying to achieve and how to achieve what we want, but using this method, you should be able to do that.

You should also remember that the success or failure of your goal depends on the actions you have selected and the time you have dedicated to completing these actions. Therefore, **failure is not related to your abilities but to the fact that you have not yet found the right actions or that you are not spending enough time on these actions to achieve your goals.**

Finally, your belief can be strongly enhanced by visualizing the achievement *before* you achieve it and seeing what you have achieved in great detail and with great emotions. Most great athletes do this as part of their training because the brain does not differentiate between an activity you visualize and one you perform. Therefore, by visualizing, you have achieved your goal, your brain will create a strong reference that you can use to enhance your belief. Also, the stronger the emotion that you have achieved the goal, the stronger the belief you can achieve it.

A helpful method for visualizing your success is through **visualization meditation**. This is different from "normal" meditation – traditional meditation is when you try to be aware of the present moment, but when you use the visualization meditation method, you are creating images in your mind of how you will be and how you will feel when you achieve.

Below you can find the mindbodism visualization meditation method, using an example for someone who wants to increase his belief that one day he will be able to visit Paris:

1. Sit in a comfortable position, with your eyes closed. You can sit on a chair, on a mat with your legs crossed, or you can lie down on the mat.

2. To enhance your experience, use a noise cancellation headset and choose music that will relate to your experience. For this example, we will find a selection of French singers, like Edith Piaf or Charles Aznavour.

3. As you inhale, lift your hands from the side to the top of your head until your palms connect, hold it for one second, and then exhale, bringing your connected palms in front of your chest and keeping your eyes closed.

4. Continue inhaling and exhaling deeply for two more breaths, and then resume normal breathing.

5. Begin to visualize having achieved what you want in great detail, using your five senses. If you do not have enough references, you can easily search for them on the Internet before you start the visualization method. In our example, if the man has never been to Paris, he could look at travel guides or videos of the places he could visit in Paris, and during his visualization meditation, he will be in these places.

6. Start the visualization using all five senses. For example:

> It is a sunny morning, and I am walking on the little streets of Sacre Coeur. I cannot believe I have finally made it to Paris, but I am here. I am walking down the street and can see the little bakery and cafes. I can see the street artists wanting to make a painting for me. I stop in front of the bakery, and I can smell the warm croissants that one can smell from far away.

> I enter the bakery and order a croissant from an old lady with a smile on her face. As I bite into the croissant, I can hear the crunchy noise and taste the buttery explosion in my mouth. I'm so happy – how can a small bite of a croissant make me so happy?

After finishing the visualization meditation, do a small positive affirmation: *I believe I can be in Paris. I have faith, so it is only a matter of time until I am in Paris.*

Slowly open your eyes and give a big smile, feeling happy at having achieved what you wanted.

This method can also be used to enhance your beliefs and adjust your mood and make you feel happy. So next time you have negative emotions, try to use the visualization meditation method and think of a place, a moment, or a person that made you feel good.

Finally, creating a vision board is another method of enhancing your belief and becoming more self-confident. A vision board is where you list all your goals but replace the words with pictures. For example, if I want to buy a car, I will put the image of the car I want to buy on the board. As they say, a picture is worth a thousand words, and it is easier to visualize and remember your goal with an image.

Here is the mindbodism vision board method:

1. List the goals you want to achieve. We always like balance, so we recommend creating goals in these categories: self-development, health/fitness, relationships, financial/business, and material (i.e., things you want to buy). Also, enhance your vision board by having a positive affirmation that will connect to a higher purpose, like the examples below.

2. For **self-development**, if you want to learn how to play the piano, put a picture of a great pianist like Sergei Rachmaninoff. Or, if you want to become a ballerina, put a picture of Anna Pavlova. Then add a positive affirmation such as *I practice daily, and one day I will be as good as Sergei Rachmaninoff, so I can entertain and give happiness to people when they listen to me playing the piano.*

3. For **health/fitness,** put a picture of the ideal body you want to have or a great athlete like Michael Jordan, and add a positive affirmation like *I eat healthy food, and I exercise every day because I want to live longer and help humanity for a longer time.*

4. For **relationships,** put a picture of you and the person you want to improve a relationship with and add a positive affirmation such as *I'm a great husband,* and *I have the most perfect and loving and caring relationship in the world.*

5. For **financial/business,** put a picture of someone you think is successful in business, like Warren Buffet, and add a positive affirmation such as *I am a very successful entrepreneur, and the companies I build will help people and make the world a better place.*

6. For **material,** put a picture of something you want to buy, such as your dream house or car, and add a positive affirmation like: *I will have a house on a Greek island and spend the summer there with my family, as I always want to provide what is best for them.*

7. Once you create the vision board, you should spend a few minutes with it when you wake up and before you go to bed. Continuous visualization and manifestation will increase your confidence and belief that you can achieve what you want, and you will be able to start and finish your day happy. As we have discussed, in terms of the good feeling you are getting, the reward chemical in your brain does not recognize whether you are thinking something or performing the activity.

Note: This book's vision board and affirmations are just mindbodism recommendations. You should personalize them to have a more significant impact on your life.

To summarise, if you want to strengthen your belief, then do the following:

1. **Create positive affirmations and have faith.**

   I believe I can achieve anything I want. I have faith, so I know it is only a matter of time until I achieve what I want. I believe that with my continuous actions, my life will change completely, I will transform into the person I want to become, and I will be able to achieve anything I want. I believe in my abilities, and I have faith. I can feel the change happening in me; I am confident and powerful and ready to achieve anything I want.

2. **Break your bigger goals down into smaller goals and think 1+1=2.**

   Find the relationship between your actions and your goal. Tackle the low-hanging fruit first. If you do not reach your goal, change your actions or spend more time on them. Complete the actions with low effort but High Impact first.

3. **Use visualization meditation.**

   Create images in your mind of how you will be and what you will feel when you achieve using your five senses.

4. **Use a vision board.**

   List your goals by replacing words with images in all development areas and adding an affirmation that focuses on a higher purpose.

STEP 2: **MASTER YOUR INNER VOICE**

Mastering your inner voice will allow you to eliminate excuses and find motivation from within.

We now strongly believe that we can achieve our goal because we believe in it and have faith, but there is an inner voice in our head that does not let us start because that voice always finds millions of excuses for why we should not start now.

Have you ever found yourself trying to wake up in the morning but hearing an inner voice telling you to go back to bed? Or have you tried to complete something, postpone it, but have time to complete the easy and unimportant tasks? Why is that? What is this voice that tells you to stay where you are, not spend your energy trying to change and avoid risks?

Your inner voice is the translation of your thoughts into muted speech. Being aware of the voice is very important because it speaks to you and influences your actions. However, if you are used to speaking in a certain way, then it requires effort to change how you speak. Therefore, you need to learn how to talk again, using words that will move you forward and ask the right questions to bring you closer to your goal.

First of all, it is not a bad thing to have inner voices; these will help you when you make decisions. They will prevent you from doing something that can potentially harm you or put you at risk, and they will help you to do something you have never done before. So, it is a matter of learning how to master these voices and direct them toward a positive outcome, helping you choose the actions that will bring you closer to your goal. You can imagine these voices as your two life coaches, sitting across from each other and giving you advice. One life coach will advise you to take action to achieve your goals, and the other will recommend you choose the action that is easy and unrelated to your goal.

**To master the inner voices,
we first need to become aware of them.**

The easiest way to be aware of the inner voice is by asking yourself the question, **"What am I thinking?"** and then providing an answer. You will see a conversation inside your mind asking questions and answering – this is your inner voice.

Practising mindfulness is the best way to become aware of your inner voice. Mindfulness is the type of meditation in which you try to be fully aware of the present moment. When you practice mindfulness, you need to let your inner voice and thoughts pass in front of you like clouds, without judging or paying any attention to them. In that way, the next time a thought tells you not to follow your goal, you must let it go, like a cloud passing in front of you, and take the action you need to achieve what you want. When you master mindfulness, you will do the action using your subconscious mind without even having to think or doubt. It will be like when you are thirsty and have your glass of water in front of you. You do not need to think about picking up and drinking from the glass; you just do it.

So, if your goal is to wake up early, when you wake up, you will start doing it without having any doubts. It is like when you bring two magnets close together. If the magnets had minds, they would not think that they need to connect with each other, but if you bring them close together, they will automatically connect.

To practice mindfulness, you can try one of the mindbodism methods below:

The Light

1. Wear comfortable clothes and lie down on a mat with your back and your palms facing up.

2. To enhance your experience, use noise cancelation headphones and find a 432 Hz meditation sound.

3. Close your eyes and take a deep breath in through your nose, holding it for one second and then exhaling through your mouth. Do this three times until you are fully relaxed.

4. Imagine there is a bright warm light touching the top of your head. As the light touches you, it will generate more heat and slowly move toward your forehead. Now you are paying attention to your forehead muscles – observe them relax as the light now brightens that area.

5. The light will continue down, brightening and softening the muscles of your eyes, nose, lips, tongue, and chin. Now your head is completely relaxed and bright.

6. Then the light will start moving down further, touching your neck and releasing any tension or stress that may have accumulated there. You will feel the warmth of the light as it touches any area where you feel more tension.

7. The light will move toward your shoulders, touching your biceps, triceps, back, and chest. These will then be relaxed and warm as well.

8. Then, your belly and lower back will start to warm, especially in areas where you may experience pain or tension.

9. The light will continue to your genitals and bottom, and everything will begin to feel relaxed.

10. As the light moves through your legs, calves, and feet, the light will make these areas bright and warm.

11. At this point, your body should be completely relaxed, warm, and bright. Now, stay there and just observe your thoughts without judgment. None of your thoughts can harm you or cause fear or stress. These thoughts are just there to observe. They come and go like waves in the sea.

12. Once you are fully aware of your thoughts and you want to stop the exercise, you can slowly open your eyes, stretch yourself like you are just waking up, and then stand.

This is a beneficial exercise of being mindful. The more you practice, the better you will recognise when your inner voice is trying to stop you from achieving your goal.

There is also a faster mindfulness method, using the Power of One Second:

One Second

Using the Power of One Second as a trigger, say: *I am mindful of my inner voice.*

Now pay attention to your inner voice if you believe it. This method can have multiple applications, and the more you practice, the more you will be able to be mindful. For example, you could say, "I am mindful of eating," and then try to be aware of what you see every time you take a bite: the smell, the sound, the taste. Or, as you say, "I am mindful of walking," then pay attention to your five senses. Pay attention to your breathing and see how it makes you feel, how it changes your mood, and how your body moves when inhaling and exhaling as you say, "I am mindful of breathing."

As you can see, the applications are endless, so find one that you like to practice. This method can also help you concentrate by saying, *I am now focused; I eliminate any distractions.*

A helpful tip to help you be mindful is to slow down the time. For example, instead of eating quickly, try to eat as slow as you can. That will help you focus more on the activity you are doing. Similarly, try to walk slowly and observe everything around you – you will see that it is like walking in a new place. Find your own applications and see how it goes.

After practicing mindfulness and becoming more able to listen to and interact with your inner voice, you will see it will ask you questions and challenge you not to do things. The inner voice will tell you it is not the right time to take action: *do not do it, you cannot do it.* When you stop accepting what the voice tells you, you will be capable of replying and showing your inner voice that is wrong. Then you will start to see the difference.

So, next time your inner voice asks you not to do something and wants to keep you in your comfort zone and prevent you from reaching your goals, try to say this:

No excuses, I must do it.

Think about your why and what are you trying to achieve, and use the Power of One second to do it.

Replace any negative words that the inner voice suggests, like "cannot," with positive words like "can do."

For example, if you have set a time to work on your business idea, your inner voice might be lazy and tell you that you do *not* have to do it now and that it would be better to watch TV instead. You need to become aware that the voice's advice will not help you reach your goals. Think with the Power of One Second and reply that you will work on the business idea because you have a strong belief and a strong why – and then do it.

The fact that you are not giving in to the initial inner voice also enhances your willpower, which is your ability to resist short-term temptations to meet your long-term goals.

The more frequently you face this challenge and choose the action that will bring you closer to your goals, instead of choosing the easy unrelated action, the stronger your willpower will become, and the closer you will get to your goal.

You can also generate this challenge instead of waiting for it to come to you. For example, when your goal is to get fit by exercising, the inner voice could tell you not to exercise, or the inner voice could tell you to stop and think with the Power of One Second and just start exercising, even for one second or one more rep. When you show your inner voice that you are in control, that will motivate you to continue. That is the Power of One Second.

The more wins you have from these challenges, the more your willpower will increase, and the closer you will be to your goal, as you are now taking actions that relate to your goal.

It is like a muscle you need to train to grow and become stronger.

You can also take an action to make it easier to win these battles with your inner voice, which is to set your environment up in the right way and eliminate any excuses.

For example, if you are struggling to start reading a book, have it next to your bed, so you can just pick it up and start reading it when can. If your inner voice says you do not have time to read it, plan to read it first thing in the morning. This way, the inner voice has fewer excuses to prevent you from doing what you need to do.

Another way to minimize the influence of your inner voice is to use the Japanese technique *poka yoke*, which means mistake-proofing. With this technique, you will try to design a process that will prevent you from making mistakes – or, in our case, prevent you from performing actions that will lead you away from your goal. For example, if you want to stop eating chocolate, and the chocolate is in a place that is easily accessible, your inner voice will most likely tell you to eat the chocolate, as it will increase your dopamine and feel good. A *poka yoke* action would be not buying the chocolate in the first place. If there is no chocolate in the house, then you cannot eat it.

To summarise:

1. **Be aware** and recognize that you have an inner voice that will sometimes try to convince you not to choose an action that will help you achieve your goal.

2. When the inner voice challenges you to follow an easy action unrelated to your goal, **think about your why** and use the Power of One Second to choose the action that impacts your goal, and then take it.

3. **Change any negative sentences** that include terms like "cannot do" to positive ones like "can do."

4. **Enhance your willpower** by challenging the inner voice that tries to stop you from reaching your goals, and remember: every battle you win is one step closer to your goal.

5. **Set up your environment** in a way that makes it easier for you to do your intended actions.

6. **Use *poka yoke*** and design a process that does not allow you to take actions that move you away from your goal.

7. **Practice mindfulness** to help you block your thoughts or help you observe your thoughts without judging or interacting.

STEP 3: MASTER THE VOICE OF OTHERS

"When there is no enemy within,
the enemy outside can do you no harm."
African proverb

Once you master how to control the inner voice, you will also need to master how to manage the voices of others. Every time we talk to someone, we are influenced in some way by what they say. Depending on how well you know yourself and how much you trust the person will affect the degree of influence they have on you. This creates a problem because we often trust the people we love, though the people we love might not be the experts on how to reach our goals, and we need to be careful.

Also, the people that love you will try to protect you and not let you get hurt, so they will most likely not challenge you or advise you to take risks and will probably have a "cannot-do" or "should-not-do" mentality. This is when you will need to ask the question, **"Is this person's advice helping me reach my goals?**

If the answer is no, you should respect their advice but ultimately ignore it. You already believe you can achieve your goal, so you should not listen to anyone who says you cannot.

Also, you will see that people's advice is often biased. It is based on what *they* think, what *they* have done, and how *they* behave. So, if they are afraid to take action or risks in their lives, they will try to pass that fear to you. Similarly, if they do not like to change, they most likely advise you not to do so, either. Therefore, ignore what they say and stay focused on your goals. If you do not believe me, then believe the following people:

Vincent Van Gogh is one of the world's most famous post-Impressionist painters, he said, "I dream of painting, and then I paint my dream." Many critics did not like his paintings because they were too dark and not very lively, and he only managed to sell one painting while he was alive, but none of that stopped him. He creates over 900 pieces of art, and today each one of them costs millions of dollars.

Walt Disney once said, "All our dreams can come true if we have the courage to pursue them." He was fired from one of his first jobs in Kansas City in 1919 because "he lacked imagination and had no good ideas." If Walt Disney had listened to others and stopped believing in himself, he would never have created The Walt Disney Company.

Before she became famous for *The Oprah Winfrey Show*, a producer once told Oprah Winfrey that she was "unfit for television." Oprah became one of America's most famous TV hosts, and an actress, producer, and philanthropist. As Oprah says, "You define your own life. Don't let other people write your script."

Elvis Presley, later known as the "King of Rock and Roll," was fired by the manager of Grand Ole Opry only after one performance. The manager said, "You ain't going nowhere, son. You ought to go back to driving a truck." If Elvis had listened, he would never have gone on to provide entertainment to millions of people. He said, "To judge a man by his weakest link is like judging the power of the ocean by one wave."

Early in her career, Meryl Streep, a future 21-time Academy Award nominee (and three-time winner), auditioned for a role in *King Kong*. The producer said to his son, "Why are you bringing me this ugly thing?" If the voice of this producer had stuck in her head, it would have prevented her from pursuing her career. In addition to the Academy Awards, she has been nominated for a Golden Globe 32 times (and has won the award eight times).

Therefore, next time you listen to someone who tries to convince you that you are not good enough to pursue your goals, remember the people above and prove them wrong. Also, if you **surround yourself with a group of friends who always supports and motivates you,** that can help you focus on what you want to achieve.

Similarly, build your network and surround yourself with people or coaches that have already achieved goals like yours, and ask them how they have done so – this can be a shortcut to your goals. The more time you spend with them, and the more time you spend discussing your goals, the faster you will get to where you want to be. Not only will you strengthen your belief that you can achieve your goal – because you see examples around you of what is possible – but based on their experiences, your mentors can also share actions and shortcuts you can take to reach your goals faster.

For example, before I started writing this book, many laughed at me. The reason for that was because I had never written a book before, English is not my mother tongue, I always had difficulty communicating, and I did not have the time to write a book, as I was working full-time, running my basketball business (basketble.com) and my mindbodism business (mindbodism.com), and just had a new-born. I proved them wrong, and I followed the Power of One Second and the guidance from this book.

You do not need to know how to do it; if you know the "foundation," you will find the way. It is only of matter of time, and remember: **Do not allow anyone to tell you what you can and cannot do.**

To summarise:

1. You can listen to other people if their advice helps you reach your goal. You can test this by asking, **"Is this person's advice helping me reach my goal?"** If the answer is no, then respect their advice but ignore it.

2. Even a **slight deviation** from your goal can impact your willpower and habit pattern, so do not do it.

3. **Surround yourself** with people who have already achieved goals like yours, and discuss your goals with them often. That will strengthen your willpower, and you might find a faster way to reach your goals.

4. As the African proverb goes, *"When there is no enemy within, the enemy outside can do you no harm."*

STEP 4: **PERSISTENCE**

"A river cuts through rock, not because of its power,
but because of its persistence."
James N. Watkins

As you can see from the quote, you do not necessarily need the power to achieve something as long as you have *persistence*. Persistence is an excellent quality for success because when you are persistent, you do not give up, and when you do not give up, you always win. When you are persistent, you know that your goal is not just a point on the map. It is a destination, and you accept the challenge to start the journey because you believe you can do it and never quit until you reach your destination.

You know that to achieve your goal, you will need to start a journey that will ultimately have many obstacles and many failures. However, you must not look at obstacles and failures like the average person. Failing is not bad or negative - how can it be bad when **failure increases your knowledge** and teaches you what you should avoid next time when trying something similar? How can failure be bad when the lessons learned from failure stick with you because you experience them, rather than reading about them in a book. How can failure be bad when it **enhances your creativity?** You will be forced to look at alternative plans and actions to succeed, as quitting is not an option.

Therefore, failure is a necessary ingredient in your journey to achieving your goal. When you try to achieve something great, you will fail at some point, but with persistence, no matter how many times you fall, you will always stand up and keep going until you reach your goal. So, remember that failure is inevitable, but success is yours if you do not stop.

When I started Basketble.com, I was alone; I had no friends. Many weeks had passed, and I was playing basketball all alone, until one day, another person walked by, saw me playing, and asked me if he could join. Since then, thousands of people have joined our basketball sessions.

The fact that I was "failing" every week did not prevent me from continuing. I knew in my heart that one-day things would change, and they did. I was persistent, and did not let failure stop me from renting the court. However, if I had discovered the 1+1=2 concept we discussed earlier, I could have reached my goal faster by advertising and promoting my session. As I said, at a point in time, your life will change in one second. But instead of waiting for that second, you can take control of your life and achieve what you want *now*. Be persistent, and do not let anything stop you.

There were also times when I would write this book daily, seven days a week, starting each day at 3:00 A.M. But then something would happen and distract me, such as injury, illness, extreme workload, etc., and I would stop for weeks. There will always be something that will distract you, and that is normal. We will all face challenges, and we as humans always like to go back to old habits. But by remembering the Power of One Second, we can change our lives now and stay true to our goals. I always returned and found my path again: I was failing but never giving up.

I previously shared Thomas Edison's quote about "failing" 1,000 times before inventing the light bulb. To become persistent, the only thing you need to do is not give up. When you face a challenge, accept it and keep going; if you get off track, just remember that with the Power of One Second, you can come back. Below are some additional examples of great people who have not let failure stop them.

Sylvester Stallone (also known as Rocky Balboa) said:

"Let me tell you something you already know. The world ain't all sunshine and rainbows; it's a very mean and nasty place, and I don't care how tough you are; it will beat you to your knees and keep you there permanently – if you let it. You, me, or nobody is going to hit as hard as life. But it ain't about how hard you hit. It's about how hard you can get hit and keep moving forward, how much you can take and keep moving forward. That's how winning is done!"

Sylvester's *Rocky* script was rejected 1,500 times, but he never abandoned his goal. Eventually, United Artists bought the script and made it into a movie, which made millions of dollars and spawned several sequels.

JK was a single mother on welfare when she wrote her *Harry Potter* novels, and even when the first book was rejected by 12 publishing houses, she did not quit. As she said, "**It is our choices that show what we truly are, far more than our abilities.**" She went on to publish seven *Harry Potter* books, in addition to other titles. In 2021, the *Sunday Times* estimated her fortune at around 820 million pounds.

Henry Ford once said, **"Whether you think you can, or you think you can't, you are right."** His businesses left him broke five times, but he went on to establish one of the biggest automotive industries in the world, Ford Motor Company.

Amelia Earhart did not have money to pay for a flight lesson, but that did not stop her. As she said, **"The most difficult thing is the decision to act – the rest is merely tenacity."** She worked several jobs and then even had to take a bus and walk four miles to get to the lesson. And even though three other women were killed attempting a solo flight across the Atlantic, that did not stop her. In 1932, she became the first woman to do it.

Before creating Alibaba, the world's largest retail company, Jack Ma failed his university exam three times, was rejected from 20 jobs (including one KFC job where they hired everyone that applied, aside from him), and was rejected by Harvard 10 times. He says, **"If you don't give up, you still have a chance. Giving up is a great failure."** He is now a billionaire and the second richest person in China.

To summarise:

1. **Never give up,** and no matter how many times you fall, you can always stand up until your reach your goals.

2. Do not let failure bring you down. See failure as a **part of the process** in order to succeed.

3. Know that people who **do not give up** always succeed because even failure is a success. Remember the Power of One Second, which is all you need to keep going.

STEP 5. **CONSCIOUSNESS**

Consciousness is a deep dive into your internal and external worlds in this second, right now. It is a laser beam focused on something you are doing now that will impact how you perceive the internal and external world. It has been a controversial subject between philosophers and scientists for many years, but I would like to explain and analyze consciousness as a tool for achievement.

We have created three levels of consciousness. The first is when you become aware of something; the second is where you are not only aware of something, but you experience it with your senses, and the third level is where you become one with the universe.

Let's take an example of a rose. I am outside in a garden, and I see a rose. At that moment, I have consciousness: I am aware that there is a rose in the garden. If I approach the rose and I start looking at it in more detail – such as smelling it, touching it, and looking at how it is constructed – I am in full consciousness. The highest consciousness is when I am one with everything, including the rose, and cannot be explained. It can only be understood by direct experience and will be explained in more detail in my second book, *My Spiritual Reality*. The closest experience to oneness is unconditional love. Even modern quantum physics discusses a unified field, which connects everything but of which there is no current scientific evidence.

No matter what level of awareness you experience, it is a powerful tool to achieve what you want. If you want to make money, then be **money-conscious**. If you want to save time, then be **time-conscious**. If you want to improve your relationships with others, then be **people-conscious**, and if you want to improve your health, then be **health-conscious**. If you combine consciousness with the 1+1=2 concept, then you will see how you can achieve anything you want.

Consciousness is such an important tool because it creates a laser beam focus, which can lead to better concentration and productivity. Also, by being more conscious, you will start to understand in more depth how the world is constructed around you. You will be able to be more creative and combine the knowledge and create new associations in your brain to achieve what you want. Also, you will feel happier, because you will appreciate things more.

Your self-awareness will also increase, which means you can make better decisions as you can understand your strengths and weaknesses and try to disengage from the ego that many times hold you back or guide you in the opposite direction of reaching your goal.

Raising my consciousness has helped me significantly in many areas of my life, and it has helped me succeed. By removing the ego, you increase consciousness and empathy, which results in better and stronger relationships with family and clients. Also, by raising your consciousness, you focus on others, and you try to find ways to understand and help them as you stop focusing on what you want. This gives you a greater sense of purpose and value in your life.

One of the reasons that I created mindbodism.com was to help people become healthier, happier, and more successful. I also changed the strategy for my basketball business, so instead of promoting only my sessions, I have started promoting those of others and helping people who want to create their own.

**Increase your consciousness,
and you will find a bigger and more meaningful purpose.**

Below are some practical examples of how to raise your consciousness:

1. **Practice mindbodism.** Mindbodism is a new way of living your life; you can become healthier, happier, and more successful by balancing your mind, body, and spirit. There are specific workouts to help your raise your consciousness, and you can learn more on www.mindbodism.com.

2. **Meditation.** Find a location close to nature. Sit comfortably in a cross-legged position, close your eyes, control your breathing, and try to feel the environment around you. What sounds can you hear? Focus on them. Are there any mental images you can create based on what you hear (e.g., a bird singing next to you)? Can you picture the air that is running through your body?

3. **Increase your experiences.** Try to have a new experience every day. It can be something small, like changing the way you get dressed, or taking a path you have never taken, even travelling to a different country, to help raise your consciousness.

4. Be more **open-minded**. Listen more, and be open to what you see, what you hear, and the opportunities that are presented to you. In that way, as you are open, avoiding judgment can help you become more conscious.

5. **Be present.** Try to be present more often by slowing down your movements and giving them your complete focus. Not only will you become more aware, but it can help you feel better because you can also express gratitude. For example, when you are eating, try to feel the food you eat: chew slowly, and be more aware of what this food gives you and how it makes you feel.

6. **Remove your ego.** By removing your ego, you will become more conscious because you will stop paying attention to only what you want or feel but also to your environment, and to other people. You will start noticing things that you did not see before. This will bring you closer to them, make you more connected, and create business opportunities, as you will try to satisfy other people's needs.

7. Practice **reflection**. Daily reflection not only in your consciousness but also increases your performance. Write down a few questions that you would like to reflect on, and then answer them. You can set your own questions, but some useful questions you can use are the following:

   a. Is there something blocking my progress?

   b. Did I have a new experience today?

   c. Is there something I could have done differently today?

To summarise:

1. **Consciousness** is a deep dive into your internal and external world in this second, right now.

2. **Becoming conscious** can increase performance, reduce stress, increase creativity, increase self-awareness, and increase concentration.

3. You can **expand your consciousness** by practicing mindbodism and meditation, gaining new experiences, becoming more openminded, removing your ego, being present, and practicing reflection.

5.
Create Energy to Start

If nothing can move without energy, then you need the energy to move towards your goal. Using the Power of One Second can create what you need to start.

I know some physicists reading the title of this chapter might complain that it violates the first law of thermodynamics, and they are right because the law of conservation of energy states that energy cannot be created or destroyed.

The reason I use the term "create energy" is because you are the one who is going to find the energy and use it to achieve your goal. Energy is closely related to effort, so the more energy or effort you make, the faster you will get to your goal – but only if you apply the 1+1=2 concept. Even if you put a lot of effort into achieving something, unless the actions you take affect your goal, you will never be able to get there. Hence the 1+1=2 concept and why you must master the "foundation" section of this book.

I really liked *Grit* by Angela Duckworth. In her book, she tells a story about how she was running every day, but she is not seeing any progress. After speaking to a Swedish psychologist named Ericsson, however, she discovered she was not improving because she was not doing "deliberate practice." This type of practice is essential, but unless you follow the 1+1=2 concept, which is to find the variables (actions) that influence your goal, you will still not be able to get there.

So how can you create energy to start moving towards your goals and achieve anything you want? Below you will find some techniques to help you create that energy.

1. THOUGHTS

*"If you don't control what you think,
you can't control what you do."*
Napoleon Hill

Did you know that thoughts generate energy? Actually, the energy of thoughts are photons, which are the particles of light that we can find in the stars and in the sun. The amount of energy is directly proportional to the photon's electromagnetic frequency, which means the higher the photon's frequency, the higher its energy. This also means that certain types of thoughts will generate more energy than others. Thoughts consume energy; did you know that chess grandmasters can burn 6,000 calories a day by just sitting down and thinking?

Since the energy cannot be destroyed, the energy that is generated by our thoughts can be used to take action. Both bad and good thoughts can produce energy, however, so you will need to guide your thoughts in the right way to produce the actions that will help you reach your goals.

I remember when I read Robin Sharma's book *The 5:00 A.M. Club,* I tried to follow his advice and wake up at 5:00 A.M. It seemed like an impossible task because I never used to wake up early. However, what I have done is concentrate my thoughts on a positive outcome, which involved using the Power of One Second to convince myself it only takes one second to wake up. If you think something is easy to do, then you have more chances to try it than if you think something is very difficult.

Also, because we do not think the same way each day, I have also found helpful to think that I have a challenge I need to overcome. If you think you will do it only for five days, just to overcome the challenge, that can also motivate you and create energy to begin. If you can finish the five-day challenge, your dopamine, the reward chemical, will increase, giving you a boost of happiness. Also, you will get increased dopamine every day during the challenge, just from the anticipation of your achievement.

Therefore, next time you want to create energy to start, remember that it only takes one second to start, and then just start.

Also, you can take a deep breath, smile, lift your hands up like a runner when finishing his run, believe, say *I can do it,* and then start. It will only take a second, but if you are focused, that second can be the difference between action and inaction. By taking this action, you will bring yourself closer to your goal.

2. MUSIC

"Where words fail, music speaks."
Hans Christian Andersen

Listening to music is a great way to create energy. If you want to relax, you can put on relaxing music. If you want to exercise, put an up-tempo track to raise your heartbeat or change your breathing. Music generates energy because it has the ability to engage the sympathetic nervous system – when the system is activated, it prepares the body for action, and we can use it to perform the action we want.

I have participated in many sports throughout my life, and I have always used music to create energy to start my workouts. If I'm sitting down and I am tired, I put on "Eye of the Tiger" from *Rocky II*. I will automatically stand up and practice my boxing moves on my punch bag or in the air, even if only for a few minutes. If I play basketball, and I listen the song "In the Zone," I will feel the energy in my body and practice harder. If I want to relax, I will listen to binaural relaxing beats or classical music Satie's "Gymnopedie No. 1," Debussy's "Reverie," or Brahm's "Symphony No. 3 in F. The music will sync with me and will automatically create a relaxing mood.

Think of music as another jump-start you can use to start doing something. Not only can it help you start, but it can also help you perform better. Michael Phelps, who has won the most Olympic medals, revealed that he listens to Eminem and EDM before a competition.

3. STRONG EMOTIONS

It is not the type of emotion that is important, but instead how you use it to achieve what you want. Positive and negative emotions generate energy, and it is up to you to direct this energy to achieve anything you want.

Strong emotions like love, hate, joy, fear, sexual desire, and anger can produce great energy. However, one would think that we can only use the energy of our positive emotions – like joy and love – to initiate an action that will help us reach our goals. However, negative emotions – such as fear and anger – can also be used to achieve our goals because they also create significant energy.

Let's look at an example of positive emotion, such as love. If your wife or child were in danger, you would not think twice about helping them and would not think about whether what you are doing could endanger your own life or not.

Love creates unbelievable energy that can sometimes be almost super-human. For example, In June 2009, two mothers lifted a 1.1-ton car because an eight-year-old boy was trapped underneath it. And no, they were not weight-lifting champions. Another example is the building of the Taj Mahal, which was built as a mausoleum for Mughal emperor Shah Jahan's wife, who had died in childbirth.

What actually happens in the brain, according to Richard Schwartz and Jaqueline Olds, is that love deactivates the neural pathway responsible for negative emotions, especially fear and social judgment, which can prevent you from getting started in achieving your goals. Do it for love, and you will see it will not only be easier to start but also to continue until you have reached your goal.

The same applies to you. If you find an activity, or even the anticipation of it, joyful, you can often start without any effort. What I have found is that even though I struggle to wake up early in the morning when I know I have to wake up to go on holiday, not only am I excited to wake up early, but I also sometimes even find it hard to go to bed. Associate the action you want to start with something joyful, and you will see it will be easier to begin. The more positive associations you make with the action, and the more times you repeat them, the easier it will be to get started. You can use the Power of One Second to do it. So, next time you want to start something, **remember the Power of One Second, and in one second, associate a positive outcome to the action you want to start – and then start.**

Similarly, negative emotions, such as fear or anger, can also produce great energy. For example, fear of failure can generate huge energy, which can automatically block any action against that fear. For example, if you want to start a new business, the fear of failure can stop you from even researching the business you want to create. However, you can change that in one second.

We have given so much emphasis to the "foundation" because by associating the action to your goal that is linked to a positive outcome, you will be able to sacrifice what your mind perceives as **short-term pain** for **long-term gain** and start now.

If you want to change your life, you need to answer the question, *what am I doing about it?* If you are not doing anything, then you know that your life is not likely to change any time soon.

Of course, we are humans, and what works now, will not always work because we are not always willing to follow. Sometimes we want to have the upper hand and not do what other people tell us to do, but we want to feel we have control of our own destiny.

Also, how much excitement will life give us if we only operate as robots? We are very complex organisms that are influenced by the environment, and we need different things at different times. We are like phenomena in nature, which are complex and, most of the time, non-linear. This is one of the reasons why the Power of One Second is so powerful: you can always find your way back. Every time I follow step five from the foundation section, and I find I am off-track from my goal, in one second, I will be back, and in one second, I will start again the actions I need to complete. You are not alone in this journey; we all face our own challenges, and we all have difficult actions to complete to achieve what we want. **But we are all going to be winners if we do not quit and if we keep going.**

There is a technique I have developed to turn your negative emotions into positive ones and to make you take the actions that will help you achieve your goal. For this exercise, you need to think of fire. Your negative emotions are like fire – you can use them to keep you warm, lighten your path or burn you. So, next time you have negative emotions, be aware of the fire and think about how you can use it to start or do something positive.

To help you do that, you also need to understand *why* you are feeling that way and to understand that just by saying why – even if the reason is silly – you can do the action you want.

There was an experiment which was conducted by Dr. Ellen Langer, a Harvard psychology professor, on a group of students found that when a student explained the reason *why* she wanted to jump the queue to make a photocopy, more than 90 percent of the students let her jump the queue, even when she said, "May I get in front of you to make photocopies because I want to make photocopies?" However, when she gave no reason, only 44 percent of the students let her jump the queue. This is also one of the reasons why, when there is a delay in the London Underground, they always try to explain why, so the passengers will be able to manage their negative emotions better, usually anger for being late at work.

But how does this apply in practice? Below is one of the applications I am using to transform negative emotions into an action I need to take to achieve my goal.

First, I understand that I am responsible for my future, emotions, and actions. I also know that, like fire, I can guide my negative emotions to produce something positive. Before I started writing this book and researching on how to achieve anything I wanted, I let my negative emotions prevent me from taking action.

In particular, I had an 11-month-old son who always woke up at night. Initially, when I was waking up at 3:00 am, sometimes I felt angry because he was disturbing my sleep, and then I was giving the excuse that I was too tired to focus on writing this book or working on my business. However, I decided to try to understand why I was feeling that way. And one of the books that helped me understand it was by reading Eckhart Tolle's book *The Power of Now*.

Since then, I have realized that I was putting myself above my son, and I was letting my ego create the emotion of anger. Once I became aware of that, I changed the narrative and flipped my ego to create a positive emotion instead. It was easy and effective.

Initially, my narrative was "my son does not let me sleep." Then my narrative changed: "my son needs my help." Can you see the difference? In one second, your emotions can change just by changing your narrative. When your emotions change, your actions change as well. By understanding how my ego works, I changed my narrative, and I used the same ego to create positive emotions.

And that was not the only positive change that was happening. As I had to wake up to feed my son and now had positive emotions, my mind looked at how it could help me achieve my goal, which was to write my book. How could this create energy to make me start writing my book? And as soon as I asked myself this question, I realized that I could continue my research while I was awake by listening to audiobooks – instead of reading them, I could listen to them, so I gained time. Also, after putting my son back to bed with the Power of One Second, I started my day early, at 3:00 A.M., and continued writing the book instead of going back to sleep.

It is amazing how you can change your actions by switching your emotions and that you can see that this transformation is all within you. You just need to use the negative emotions in a way that can help you start the action you want to take. So, next time you have a negative emotion:

1. Understand you are responsible for your future, emotions, and actions.

2. Become aware of your negative emotions.

3. Think that, like fire, you can use negative emotions to benefit you, like keeping you warm, lighting your path or burning you.

4. Understand why you feel this way.

5. Change your narrative to create a positive emotion.

6. Think of an action you can start to help you achieve your goal.

7. Act now.

8. Reflect on how mastering this technique can help you in your journey.

There is a powerful *one-second* trigger you can use when you have negative emotions: **SMILE.** When you feel stressed, when you face difficulties, when you are upset, just smile, and it will melt any negative emotions. There is also a mindbodism practice, called the "healing smile," that you can use. You can find this practice at www.mindbodism.com.

Another technique to help you transform negative energy into positive action is imagining you are a martial artist. If you have studied or watched some Wing Chun or Aikido movements, you have seen that competitors take the opponent's momentum and energy and transform them into positive energy, which they then use to throw the opponent on the floor. In the same way, every time you have negative energy or negative emotions, become aware of them and transform them into something positive or to your advantage, just like they do in martial arts.

Negative associations can also have the same effect. For example, suppose you associate something as being bad, and you are experiencing it on a daily basis. In that case, there will be a point at which you will have accumulated too many negative emotions for an action to be initiated—in this particular example, raising your awareness is again important, because like fire, they can keep you warm or they can burn you.

Suppose you have a goal to improve your health by eating well. If you let yourself get carried away and eat lots of junk food, there will be a point at which you will start feeling poorly. If this is how you feel daily, it can lead you to feel bad, or it can motivate you to start exercising and eating healthily. Personally, I used this technique when I tried to stop eating chocolate. What I used to do was to try to eat five chocolates until I felt I had enough to make me start a healthy diet the next day. I know many people who have stopped smoking and stopped drinking because one day, they felt they had had enough, or they felt a lot of pain from smoking or drinking.

Finally, a negative emotion like fear can be used to create energy and start doing something that will help you reach your goals. However, you need to understand that fear is wired into your DNA. Long ago, when you think that you are threatened either physically or psychologically, it triggers one's fight-or-flight response, and long ago, that was necessary for your survival.

Both Mahatma Gandhi, Warren Buffet had a fear of speaking in public, but both of them were able to overcome the fear and use it to take action to reach their goals.

Mahatma Gandhi, one of the greatest political and spiritual leaders of the twentieth century, was once unable to complete a speech given to a vegetarian community in London because of his fear. He was only able to read only one sentence before asking someone else to complete his speech. However, his desire to set India free, made him overcome his anxieties and fears and later speak to thousands.

Similarly, at the age of 19, Warren Buffet, later one of the wealthiest people in the world, was afraid to speak in public. However, that did not stop him; he used his fear to create energy and enroll in a public speaking course, which eventually helped him overcome his fear and become a successful public speaker. He did not let the negative emotions stop him from achieving his goals, and used them to create positive action.

As we have discussed earlier, there are many types of fear, but as you can see, you can always use them to your advantage to create energy and start something. No matter what kind of fear you are experiencing, you will realize that in most cases, the magic ingredient is practice.

If you are afraid of public speaking, enroll in a course, or start speaking to a small group of people. If you are afraid of starting your own business, start by creating a simple product or service and try to sell it. If you are afraid to change, make a small change until you can confidently move to a bigger one.

4. LEARNING

"If you are not willing to learn, no one can help you. If you are willing to learn, no one can stop you."

Zig Ziglar

Reading a book, taking a class, or watching videos related to the goal you want to achieve can also create energy. You can use this energy to start the actions that will help you reach your goal. Because every bit of new information you learn creates new associations in your brain, it can increase your belief that you can also do it. It is also one of the ways that will help you discover the actions that influence your goals, which is required to master the 1+1=2 concept we discussed earlier. There are examples of many people who have spent a significant amount of time reading books. Warren Buffet still spends around five to six hours of his time reading each day, Bill Gates reads around a book a week, and Elon Musk used to read ten hours a day.

Start reading a book, and you will get the energy you need to make a start.

Many people might struggle to find time to read a book, but where there is a will, there is a way, and it is up to you to find the way.

Study not to learn but to understand, because the knowledge you cannot apply is like you have a power you cannot use. One of the tactics I use is not actually reading a book but listening to it instead. This is a great hack, and I was able to go from reading from one book a year to three books a week.

How could I do that? The most important thing to do is to understand when you are not productive and think of activities you can do while listening to a book. Driving or using public transport, exercising, or putting my son to sleep – for me, all these activities can be enhanced by listening to an audiobook. You will be amazed at how fast you can finish a book. You can also create more time by increasing the speed of listening.

In that way, you can even spend half of the time required to listen to an audiobook by speed listening. Speed-listening works best when you are actually focused on listening to the audiobook without any distractions.

Similarly, I know that some people prefer to read a book, so those of you should try speed-reading. Again, you will be amazed at how fast you can read when you master this technique. Of course, I am not asking you to become Howard "Speedy" Berg, who can read 80 pages per minute, but if you do a page in less than a minute, you are on the right track.

I learned speed-reading while doing my master's degree in Business Administration (EMBA) in London, which helped me significantly. I was able to work full-time at General Electric and still finish my MBA with merit. Here are some simple steps you can follow to improve your speed-reading techniques:

1. Focus on your reading, and do not allow anything to distract you.

2. Do not say the words aloud in your head as you read because that will slow you down. Just pass the words with your eyes and even read three to five words at once.

3. Do not re-read any word or sentence; always move forward.

4. Use your finger as a guide. Start by moving from left to right, and then slowly increase the speed.

5. Once you master that, try to glance at the line and then move your finger down to the middle of the page.

6. Set a goal of reading more than a page in a minute, and see how you are doing.

7. Practice, practice, practice, and you will be able to read more than a page in a minute within the first hour you apply this technique. If not, practice more.

Bonus: Once you practice and master this method, you can read a whole book and understand the main points just by scanning each page and putting an emphasis on a few keywords you read on each page.

5. SHARING WITH SOMEONE

*"Only surround yourself with people
that will lift you higher."*
Oprah Winfrey

If you want to start doing something, but find you do not have the energy, you can use another person's energy. And, following Oprah's quote, you need to find the person who will lift you higher. The individual who can help you get closer to your goal. Once you find the person, you will realize that they will create the energy to make you start. If you cannot start by yourself, then why not start with someone else?

For example, if you want to start going to the gym, why don't you invite a friend to go with you? If there are days that you might not feel like going to the gym, having someone to train with can always create energy and push you to do so. Because you are sharing this activity with someone, you do not feel alone, and you start seeing the activity as fun rather than something you need to do.

One study from the journal of consulting and clinical psychology showed that people who started a weight loss program with a friend had a 96 percent chance of completing it compared to 76 percent for those who started on their own. Even hanging around people that have achieved your goal can be the motivating factor to start the actions you need to succeed and drive you closer to your goal. A 2016 study on obesity showed that people who stayed with friends that exercise are more likely to continue losing weight. Perhaps because of peer pressure, they will want to feel valued and accepted by their friends.

Even though there are examples of companies that were started with a friend and failed, there are also examples of success stories. Sharing your vision with someone else can create the energy you need to start because you will feel like you have someone else to support you. Also, the sum is always greater than its parts, so two brains can create something bigger than two individual brains.

Airbnb and Ben and Jerry's are such examples. Nathan Blecharczyk, the co-founder of Airbnb, moved to San Francisco and found a roommate, Joe Gebbia. Then when he moved out, a friend of Joe's, Brian Chesky, moved in. In 2008, all three became close friends, and one day, when there was a shortage of hotels in San Francisco, they decided to create a website to rent spaces in people's homes. This led to the creation of Airbnb.

Similarly, Ben Cohen and Jerry Greenfield, friends since the seventh grade, created their first ice cream shop in Burlington, Vermont, in 1978. Since then, their company was bought by Unilever, and the ice cream is now sold worldwide. Also, as we have mentioned before, life will give you what you need, not what you want. Cohen, for example, had severe anosmia, and his lack of smell led to the company's trademark chunks being mixed with ice cream.

Personally, I have used this method for activities such as exercising or starting a healthy diet. For example, my best friend, Dennis and I, go to a local gym and exercise every morning. Also, when I want to start a healthy diet, I always start it with my wife, which not only improves our health but also our relationship, as we are doing something together.

6. EXERCISING

"I hated every minute of training, but I said, 'Don't quit. Suffer now and live the rest of your life as a champion.'"
-Muhammad Ali

You are probably asking how exercise can create energy, as it usually consumes energy. However, according to Dr. Tony Golen and Hope Ricciotti, editor-in-chief of *Harvard Women's Health Watch*, exercising can give you more energy because it helps your body produce more mitochondria, which in turn increases your body's energy supply. Furthermore, exercising improves oxygen circulation in your body, which can help your body operate better and more efficiently.

Another reason exercise creates energy is because it improves your mood and decreases feelings of depression and anxiety. Also, it increases the brain sensitivity hormones serotonin and norepinephrine, which relieve the feeling of depression. Furthermore, exercising can increase the production of endorphins, which are associated with positive emotions. Therefore, if you wake up and exercise, you will feel much better, which can create the energy to do the activities that will help you reach your goals. This is why if you have exercised at night, you may feel more energetic and less able to sleep.

You should not give yourself any excuses for not being able to exercise. Even a ten-minute walk can lower cholesterol, improve concentration, burn calories, reduce stress, and clear your mind.

I have been exercising and doing sports all my life, and I think this is one of the reasons I am rarely sick and always have a positive mindset. In addition, being an athlete helps me overcome my life challenges and have more endurance. My favourite exercise routine is waking up early in the morning and doing a twenty-minute, full-body, high-intensity training while listening to audiobooks. That way, I can start my day full of energy while also exercising my mind and developing myself.

However, depending on your goals – like weight loss, muscle growth, and so on – you will need to choose the right exercise program. Remember that 1+1=2, and even though you exercise, if you do not find the relationship between the exercises you do and the goal you want to achieve, you will never be able to reach your goal. Normally for weight loss, you need to do more repetition and cardio, but if you want to build muscle and get stronger, you usually do fewer repetitions but with heavier weights. You can find more information online, or you can set an appointment with a personal trainer to see how you can achieve your goal.

Also, I have discovered that when I exercise, I automatically tend to eat healthier and do not crave food that is bad for my health. Then, I did some research, and I found a 2015 publication from the *Journal of American College Nutrition* that explained the reason you tend to eat healthier when exercising regularly is the "transfer effect." The transfer effect occurs when learning a new skill, information, or attitude, such as exercising, which is transferred to a second behavior, such as eating.

Many successful people like Barack Obama, Ariana Huffington, and Bill Gates have the habit of exercising in the morning. Barack Obama usually completes a 45-minute training session in the gym, focusing on strength conditioning and cardio training. Sometimes he replaces the gym exercise by playing basketball or golf. Ariana Huffington starts with meditation for 20 to 30 minutes, followed by 30 minutes cycling on a stationary bike. And Bill Gates' exercise routine is spending an hour on the treadmill while watching educational courses from the Teaching Company's "Great Courses" series.

The important thing is to include in your daily routine at least 20 minutes of exercise. Then, you will see that your energy level will increase, and you will find it easier to start the actions that help you achieve what you want and bring you closer to your goal.

6.
Maintain Momentum and Never Stop

"The world is wide, and I will not waste my life in friction when it could be turned into momentum."
Frances E. Willard

In the previous chapters, you have defined your goals and started working toward them. However, we still have one last problem: often, we start something, but then we stop. This happens to all of us, but what can we do to ensure we maintain this momentum? The following actions can help you keep the momentum or find it when you have lost it.

1. RESTORE ENERGY

"May the sun bring you new energy by day. May the moon softly restore you by night. May the rain wash away your worries. May the breeze blow new strength into your being. May you walk gently through the world and know its beauty all the days of your life."
Apache Blessing

While you are working on your goal, there will be a lot of energy that you will need to consume. Identifying and implementing the actions you need to complete to reach your goal will require a lot of effort and work hours, days, or even years. Therefore, you will need to restore your energy to keep going. Otherwise, you will burn out and not be able to continue.

It is the same when you work out – if you exercise a muscle for too long and you are not careful, you can tear it and cause injury. This is very common with athletes when they stretch themselves too much and do not understand their limits. Below you can find five simple actions you can take to help you restore your energy:

1. **Take frequent breaks**: According to *Psychology Today,* taking a break directly impacts your productivity. Every person is different, so you can try different work and break patterns to see what works for you. One method I use is to work for 50 minutes and then take a ten-minute break. Make sure you use a timer, like your watch or phone. This method will not only restore your energy but will increase your focus since you have a specific time that you will need to complete the task and be more productive.

   During the ten-minute break, you can start by drinking water, followed by completing some breathing exercises. You can enhance your breaks with other activities that restore your energy, such as stretching, affirmations, going for a quick walk in nature, spending time with your family, or doing a ten-minute meditation. However, it is important to have these breaks to be balanced.

2. **Meditate:** According to a study by the *University of Waterloo*, a 25-minute mediation can improve brain function and energy levels. Personally, even ten minutes of meditation, combined with breathing techniques and Qi Gong, can restore my energy and continue the actions that will help me achieve my goals.

3. **Take a nap:** There is a lot of research on the benefits of napping. Some studies, like the one from *Nature Neuroscience*, say to take a longer nap (between 30 and 60 minutes) to be alert. Other studies, like the one from the *Mayo Clinic*, recommend only taking a ten- to 20-minute nap, as it might affect your night sleep.

   My advice is to connect with your body and feel what you need. I have taken everything from a three-minute nap up to a two-hour nap. In both cases, I have felt more alert and have had more energy. Remember that five minutes today might have a different effect than five minutes tomorrow. This is why it works best to connect with myself to see what I need. If I feel I need to take a nap but only have five minutes, I will take a five-minute nap. All this will depend on the time I have available, of course.

4. **Eat to increase energy.** Another reason why you might be tired is that you have eaten sugar. Even though a lot of people feel that eating sugar can boost their energy, according to a 2019 article in *Neuroscience and Biobehavioural Reviews*, after 30 minutes of consumption, eating sugar actually increases fatigue. However, eating foods with a low glycaemic index, such as whole grains, nuts, and high-fibre vegetables, may help you keep the energy.

   Personally, I love eating nuts. Even a handful of mixed nuts not only increases my energy but also helps me keep going when I am hungry.

5. **Drink water.** If you do not drink water, you will become dehydrated, which means your motivation will decrease and fatigue will increase. In a *Cambridge* study done in 2011, researchers found that even mild dehydration impairs cognitive performance and mood. I know the benefits of drinking water, but even as simple as it sounds, most of us do not have time to drink water. I have tried apps and set alarm clocks, but it was hard to stick to the routine. However, what has worked for me is having a bottle of water in front of me at my desk. Once it is there, I will find time to drink it. And once I drink it, I will go to fill another one.

2. ACT WITHOUT THINKING

For some, acting without thinking is insanity;
for others, it is impulsivity, but for me,
it saves energy, which can help you keep momentum.

I am not saying that we should always act without thinking, but for certain actions, if we complete them without thinking, it can save us energy and help us perform better and work for longer periods of time. We can do this because of a network of interacting brain regions that are active when a person is not focused on the outside world, called the Default Mode Network.

It is like when you drive your car. Initially, you had to think through a complex series of instructions before you started driving. However, after some time, all the steps come naturally to you, so you can start the ignition without thinking. You can save energy.

Our brain tries to work more efficiently. An October 2017 article in *Neuroscientist* described an experiment with 28 students who were asked to match their cards with new cards. Through scans, their brain activity was examined, and researchers found that the patterns of the brain resembled those of learning minds initially. However, once the students were trained, the brain patterns resembled those of Default Mode Network, and their responses were faster and more accurate. This made me realize that when you practice something a lot of times, you go into autopilot mode, which makes it easier to complete the activity.

Also, according to a 2015 article published by Gretchen Schmelzer, a psychologist trained as Harvard Medical School Fellow, repetition creates the strongest learning, as it creates a long-term memory, as strong chemical interactions connect neurons to other neurons. Now, if you combine practice and repetition, it can potentially link to your behavior, because according to Wendy Wood, a social psychologist at the University of South California, what forms a habit is repetition and reward. This is one of the reasons to create a new habit, we need to repeat it many times. But why do we need to form a habit, and how many days will it take?

According to a 2009 research article published by the *European Journal of Social Psychology,* it can take between 18 and 254 days to form a new habit and an average of 66 days for a new behavior to become automatic. We need habits, so we can stay focused on the actions that will help us achieve our goals.

For example, when I was struggling to find time to write this book, I told myself that every day at 5:00 A.M. I would sit down and write the book. That planning helped me keep focused on my task, and the repetition helped me adopt the habit of writing the book daily, even at the weekend. Also, to achieve that, I tried to eliminate any excuses, and if something happened at 5:00 A.M., like my son being up and me taking care of him, I would still write the book because I was committed to this habit. From experience, doing it later in the day made the task more challenging to complete, so it was easier to do it at the same time every day. Also, if you struggle with time, do your task first thing in the morning when you wake up.

Now forming a habit for me is a daily ritual, and I do the actions daily to help me achieve my goal. I have also found that being committed to the activity, even if I could not do it at the same time every time, created momentum and kept me motivated to continue the activity and keep going. I did research to see if there were any experiments on this and found Katie Milkman's book, *How to Change*. In her book, she describes the group of participants who, when they were more flexible about the time they were exercising, exercised more frequently than the participants that had to exercise at only a specific time each day.

But how we can develop a habit?

> *"We are what we repeatedly do.*
> *Excellence then is not an act, but a habit."*
>
> -Aristotle

As you can see, even when Aristotle was living, around 322 B.C., habit was always important to think about. More recently, a lot of research and books have been written on how to create a habit. *The Power of Habit* by Charles Duhigg, *Atomic Habits* by James Clear, *Good Habits, Bad Habits* by Wendy Wood, and many more. According to Wood, we spend around 43 percent of our day doing things without thinking about them. So, imagine what you can do if those things you do are actions to help you achieve what you want. You will get there a lot faster, as you will not have to face all the excuses for why you cannot do certain things.

According to Duhigg, people cannot create new habits because they do not understand the habit loop, which is the neurological loop of any habit and consists of the cue, response, and reward. Cue is the trigger to start a habit, the response is the action you take, and reward is the reward you receive by doing the action. In *Atomic Habits*, James Clear also explains that to create a new habit, you need to make it obvious, attractive, easy, and satisfying.

Forming a habit is important because when you have a goal, and a habit of working on your goal, success will arrive much faster. Since I have started writing this book, I have changed many habits, from the food I eat to how I get dressed, think, and create. Even though the process described below worked for me, you should experiment, as we discussed in step 5 of the foundation, and see what works for you.

Step 1: Think of a habit you want to develop. This can be exercising, reading a book, starting your own business, or waking up in the morning. Anything you want to achieve.

Step 2: Explain why. You need to be able to explain *why* you want to start a habit so that when you have doubts about if you want to continue this habit, you can always go back to your "why." The stronger and more meaningful your why, the higher the chance you will continue this habit.

Step 3: Plan. You need to plan when, where, and how to start a habit. For example, if you want to exercise, it is good to know the time/date you are going to start, such as 7:00 A.M. on Monday. Where are you going to exercise (the gym, your living room, etc.)? How you are going to exercise (what equipment or workout you are going to use?)? You also need to know what you will do *after* your workout and try to create a reward for what you did. For me, it is drinking a green tea or smoothie.

Step 4: Start. In this step, you start the action you intend to do. Start exercising, read a book, do some research on a business you want to start. Since you have everything planned and you have a strong why it is easier to start with this habit. Also, use the Power of One Second to boost action now.

Think "no excuses" and think of challenges like growth, success, and the vehicle to take you from where you are to where you want to be. From who you are to whom you want to become.

You are also starting to do the actions you have planned for after your workout as a reward, such as drinking some tea, playing with your baby, or listening to some music.

Step 5: Reflect. This is one of the most important steps because even if you have skipped steps two through four, you should always complete this one. That way, you will be able to reflect on what is working or not working and try to improve, so you will be able to stick to your habit. So, if you are not able to start a habit or continue, you need to reflect on steps two through four.

1. If you do not stick to your habit because you do not feel it is important to do the action, then reflect on Step 2 below.

2. If you do not stick to your habit because you find it too difficult to try and figure out what you have to do, then reflect on Step 3 below

3. If you do not stick to your habit because you find the action is too difficult to start, then reflect on step 4 below.

Reflecting on Step 2: Maybe you have not found a strong "why" to keep you motivated. When I started writing this book, my initial motivation was that I wanted to write a book. However, the why was not strong, so I have only written one page for three years. When I shifted my mind and thought that I wanted to help people improve and achieve their dreams in a specific time frame, then it became more meaningful, and every time I tried to avoid writing, I always went back to thinking of gratitude and being thankful that I have the skills to help people. I would realize I needed to help them, and then I would continue writing. Writing down what I wanted to achieve helped me create my goal.

> **"Dreams without goals, are just dreams."**
> Denzel Washington

Reflecting on Step 3: Maybe you have not planned things properly and have made it difficult to start, or maybe your reward is not strong enough. Before I started exercising daily, it was challenging because it would take time to decide which clothes to wear, what exercises to do, and when to wake up in the morning and start the preparation. Or even if I exercised once, I would not exercise the following day because I would think about how painful it was to find clothes and then waste ten minutes just trying to find the right workout. And I did not have any reward, so I tried something else.

Now I prepare my clothes the night before, I know what exercises to do by writing them down, and after working out, I drink tea or make a smoothie. That made me feel active and, at the same time, relaxed. By doing these small changes, I was able to stick to my daily routine and lose seven kilograms in three months.

As discussed earlier, another shortcut to this approach is to share it with someone.

I remember talking to Paul, a friend of mine, and him telling me that for many years, he had been unable to wake up in the morning to exercise. I asked him, "Are you going to start tomorrow?" Then he asked how, saying it was impossible? I told him that at 7:00 the next morning, we would exercise together over a video call and continue for five days. After that, he would do it by himself. He said okay.

Paul exercised every day for five days and continued the routine by himself. This is also why it is essential as a parent to support your kids in extracurricular activities from a young age and motivate them to start. As many Olympic gold medalists have said, they had the support of their families to start, so we need to do the same for our children.

Reflecting on Step 4: Maybe your actions are too difficult, and that is why you cannot start. Evaluate what actions you plan to do, and reflect on whether or not you need to change them. Before I started my daily habit of working on my business, I knew that I wanted to spend time doing that. I had a plan because I had listed all the actions I had to do the previous day and knew I had the reward of hugging my baby son as soon as I finished the actions.

However, after two days, I could not continue because the first day that I started working on my business, I realized that out of the 30 actions I was planning to complete, I had only completed five. The following day, the same. Actually, it was worse because my daily list was longer. Then I decided that there was no point, and I stopped for a few days.

However, when I reflected on why I had quit, I determined it was because I was creating an inevitable disappointment by having a huge list of activities that I had to complete daily and which were impossible to complete. So, what I did was only have the three most important actions on the list. Once I finished those, I could add three more. In that way, I was able to complete the activities that were planned but also boost additional rewards and motivation by completing more than the planned activities, by following that, I was able not only to complete more than five actions per day but also to stick with my daily habit.

Equally important is reflecting on what triggers you to follow a habit you are trying to remove from your life, a so-called "bad habit." Once you identify that, an easy hack to prevent you from returning to the bad habit is to replace it with a new good one and continue improving it.

For example, whenever I worked too much and found I was beginning to get tired or bored, I always visited my kitchen and ate some chocolate. Then, when I realized that I could finish a whole box of chocolate in two days, I changed my habit so that instead of eating chocolate, I was eating nuts. After further reflection, I realized that it was not because I was hungry that I wanted to eat, but because I wanted to get distracted. So, when I realized that, I replaced eating nuts with drinking water. That worked perfectly because I was already always struggling to drink water during the day, and this new habit of drinking more water would be healthier.

So, let's create a daily ritual together:

1. Choose an action you want to start daily.

(I want to…)

2. Write down why you want to start this habit

(Because…)

3. Plan when, where, and how you will do this action, and what you will do after completing it (the reward).

4. Start the action that will help you achieve your goal, but do not forget to also complete the action that will give you the reward.

5. Set a five-day target to do this activity daily. If you achieve the five days, try to increase the duration to the point that you do not have to think about it. Do not worry about how long it takes for the action to be performed without thinking because it depends on the individual. The important thing is to focus on the process.

6. Reflect to see how you are progressing and if you can stick with the habit. If you have stopped or have not started, to know what you need to change, reflect on steps two through four, as described above.

3. FOCUS ON YOUR WHY

"Man's main concern is not to gain pleasure or avoid pain, but rather to see a meaning in his life. That is why man is even ready to suffer, on the condition, to be sure, that he is suffering has meaning."

Viktor Frankl

When you feel like quitting, focus on your why. This will allow you to maintain momentum and become more resilient to pain. Viktor Frankl, a Viennese psychologist and prisoner at Auschwitz, detected that the prisoners who had a sense of purpose were more resilient to pain, such as torture and starvation. I know that wanting to quit is not the same type of pain, but having a purpose and knowing why you need to accomplish what you are trying to achieve, will make you more resilient.

Also, make things easier by focusing on your why. Don't only write it down; make a picture of it. As Albert Einstein once said, "One picture is worth a thousand words," so make a picture of your why.

When I was tired or felt like quitting writing the book, I had an image of the book cover I had created on my vision board, so it gave me the motivation to continue.

Another thing to remember when focusing on your why is not only why you are doing it and what you are trying to achieve, but also why you want to stop. As we have discussed, it is vital to reflect on your actions and your inactions and see what you can try to do to put you back on track to achieving your goals. Sometimes there is a valid reason why you have to stop, and sometimes a break is necessary to restore energy, as we discussed before.

Also, you need to be reminded that there will be obstacles and failures in your journey, but with the mindset you have created, you will only focus on the actions that will help you reach your goals. If you stop now, you can be sure you will never reach your goal.

Keep going; never stop. You cannot fail if you keep going because failure can only be assessed if you stop trying. If you keep going, every failure is just a milestone in your journey to success.

> *"Failures are expected by losers, ignored by winners."*
> Joe Gibbs

4. MEASURING PROGRESS

> *"What gets measured, gets done."*
> W. Edwards Deming

I remember when I first joined Ford Motor Company in 1997 as an intern; that was one of the quotes that everyone mentioned. I was responsible for improving the performance of a production line, and the only way I could find out if I had improved it was to measure the initial performance of the line and then measure it again after my improvement. Measuring progress is a very simple concept, but it is also valuable because it not only helps you understand where you are going and when you think you will achieve your goal but also helps you understand the 1+1=2 concept which is to identify the actions that impact your goals.

Changing your actions and measuring the impact on your goal can help you understand which actions are more important and which actions you need to focus on to achieve what you want. I have used this principle to monitor my workout, my progress in writing the book, and my advertising actions. It applies to almost everything that you want to improve.

Another reason why monitoring progress is important is that it can be an intrinsic motivating factor to keep going. This occurs when you do something because it is personally rewarding and because you have an inner drive. In his book *Drive*, Daniel Pink describes how people who are motivated by a desire to improve will constantly seek to improve. However, if the people did not know whether or not they were improving, then most likely their motivation might fade away in the future.

This is why it is essential to monitor progress; when you monitor progress and you see an improvement, then dopamine flows, which creates a positive association or rewarding experience. According to an article published in December 2011 by PMC, midbrain dopamine neurons are linked to positive motivation. And as we discussed previously, when you have a rewarding experience, the brain will likely try to repeat this action, helping you maintain momentum.

There was a period after COVID-19 hit that many people were unwilling to go back to play basketball. Since I had already booked the courts, I was losing money. However, that did not make me stop trying. I measured how many people attended a basketball session each week, and I started creating actions such as advertising, face-to-face meetings, and calling players. That helped me slowly gather players to play on each court. The fact that I could see that my actions were making a difference each week helped me maintain momentum and continue my actions.

Also, even if you do not see that you are making progress, by measuring your progress, you can see that failure is part of the process of success and create momentum by making you change your actions so you can achieve your goal.

There is a nice story I remember from Napoleon Hill's book *Think and Grow Rich* in which a person left his house to try to find gold, and the next person who lived in that house actually found the gold in that house. So do not give up easily; you have what you need, but you do not need to give up and raise your consciousness. There is no peak without a trough.

5. TALK TO YOUR BELIEVERS

*"Anything is possible when you have
the right people to support you."*
Misty Copeland

Believers are the people who have faith in your abilities to achieve your goal. It can be a coach, mentor, or advisor; it can be your mother, father, friend, or acquaintance – it does not matter. The important thing is to have someone in your circle that believes in you and can push you toward achieving your goals. This is why most athletes and other successful people have coaches to motivate them and show them how to achieve their goals.

For me, my parents have played that role from a young age. Even when they were young and struggling financially, they did everything they could to support me with my education because they believed that I could make a difference in this world. And even at this age, my mother is helping me run my basketball business and is always there to support me and advise me on anything I need.

Just talking to your believers and sharing your ideas and actions can be helpful because these individuals can provide alternative ways of doing things or ideas about ways to improve your existing actions in order to achieve your goals.

And do not think that only people who are experts in your problem can help. Having a diverse group of people, according to a January 2018 study by Boston Consulting Group, companies had 19 percent higher revenues due to innovation. Also, according to a March 2017 article published by *Harvard Business Review*, when teams are cognitively diverse, problems are solved faster. So, try to find people to support you from all different backgrounds.

To summarise:

1. **Restore energy.** Frequent breaks ensure you do not burn out.

2. **Act without thinking.** Do things on autopilot.

3. **Focus on your why.** Think about why you started.

4. **Measure progress.** See that your effort pays off.

5. **Talk to your believers.** Enhance your belief that you can still do it.

PART 3:

HOW YOU CAN ACHIEVE
WITHOUT MAKING SACRIFICES

7.
Change the View of the World

"If you change the way you look at things,
the things you look at will change."
Wayne Dyer

The view of the world is that in order to achieve something great, you need to sacrifice greatly. However, if you change how you view the world, you do not have to sacrifice anything.

You need to understand that you are responsible for your life, and you are the one that decides how to live based on what you think. If something bad happens to you, you are the one to decide if you will spend your time and energy feeling bad about what happened or feel good by focusing on how you can change your life to become better.

It is not easy to do, but it gets easier when you practice this way of thinking and believe it is possible. Many people try to prevent us from doing great things by trying to scare us, telling us that we do not have the abilities, or we should not sacrifice our lives to achieve what we want. Often, we see that these are pieces of "advice" from people who have not achieved what they wanted to in their lives and are consciously or subconsciously trying to pass their fears onto us.

However, by changing your view of the world, you will not sacrifice anything in your life. The reason for that is this: you are not going to sacrifice anything in your life if you do not think it is a sacrifice.

When you do something you love – playing your favourite sport- it is not a sacrifice because even if it requires effort, you still feel great. Because you changed your view of the world, you are now happy to do it because you anticipate that you will feel great in the end.

This is how you need to think and how you need to act to achieve what you want. If you do that, you are not going to sacrifice anything because you know what you want, and you know that by completing the actions that will help you achieve your goal, you will feel great because you will be able to reach those goals.

When you practice this way of thinking, you will see that your life will become more manageable, and you will feel happier. Even if you put forth more effort, you will feel more motivated to continue, as there is a positive association between these actions. Based on this way of thinking, you can also create negative associations with anything that will prevent you from reaching your goals, so you will be less likely to do anything that will move you away from your goal.

For example, suppose you needed to decide to complete your business plan or watch TV. If you view the world with the old way of thinking, you will feel you are sacrificing watching TV to complete your business plan. However, if you have embraced the new way of thinking, then you will consider it a sacrifice to not complete the business plan and to watch TV instead. In that way, you only sacrifice if you do the things that will not bring you closer to your goal.

Also, there is a misconception that we need to work harder to achieve what we want. This is also not true because you can do things more intelligently, so you do not have to spend as much time doing them or have other people do them on your behalf, as we will see in the following chapters.

8.
Create a Plan

"By failing to prepare, you are preparing to fail."
Benjamin Franklin

The other way to achieve what you want without making sacrifices is to create a plan. Having a plan saves you time, and you can still do the things you were doing before, plus have time to do new things.

A plan saves time because it can reduce the time we spend doubting ourselves and fighting with our inner voice. By creating a plan, we list our intended actions – what we need to do to achieve our goal – which gives us confidence that there is a way we can do it. At first, your plan can be high-level, but once you create it and learn more about the actions impacting your goals (1+1=2), you can make it more detailed.

Also, it saves time because you do not have to think about what you need to do next. Once you create a plan, you will know the actions you need to do; this is why we started by planning our daily ritual. However, at this stage, we need to create a high-level plan, so we know what approach to take to achieve our goal.

Good planning can also save you time because it can reduce your chances of failure and show you which activities need to be done first. For example, if you wanted to build a house and started by building the walls without first building the foundation, that would be a definite way to fail.

You need to review the plan regularly and update it as you will learn more about the activities you will need to complete, the availability of resources, and the time required to complete the activities.

Your high-level plan should have the following:

1. **Deliverable:** What are you trying to achieve (e.g., complete writing a book)

2. **Scope:** Defines what you are going to focus on (e.g., self-development book)

3. **Duration:** Start and finish time (e.g., January through April)

4. **Milestones:** Interim deliverables (e.g., by January, ten percent of the book will be completed, by February 50 percent of the book will be completed, by March 75 percent of the book will be completed, and by April, 100 percent of the book will be completed)

5. **Key activities:** Activities required to reach your goal and when are you planning to complete them (e.g., what type of self-development book to write by January, learn what is required to write a good book by January, define the high-level structure of the book, and the chapter titles by January, write a book by March, review and correct by April, and print book by April)

In our example, the final product should look like this:

Activities	Jan	Feb	Mar	Apr
1. Decide what type of self development book to write	▨			
2. Learn what is required to write a good book	▨			
3. Define the high level structure of the book and the chapter titles	▨		▨	
4. Write book by March		▨	▨	
5. Final review and correct				▨
6. Print book				▨

9.
Create Time

"Time is a created thing. To say,
'I do not have time' is to say, 'I do not want to.'"

Lao Tzu

When you create time, you do not have to sacrifice because now you have more time than before. But how can we create time if we only have 24 hours daily? It is simple: it starts by becoming aware of time and adding value to each second.

This is why the Power of One Second is very powerful – when you create value on each second, the value you will be able to create in one day is significantly more than what you used to produce in the same period.

First of all, to prove that you get more time by becoming aware of time, just look at your watch for five minutes. Time seems to have slowed down. Now, try to watch five minutes of your favourite TV show. Time is moving so fast that you cannot even know where the time is going. Therefore, we know that we can slow down time when we become aware of it because time is relative.

Now that you are aware of time, you need to create more of it. Since time is relative, you can only create time when you compare it to the actions you can accomplish within the same period. For example, if I was writing a book and could write ten pages a day, but now I can write 20, this means I have created time as long as the quality remains the same.

However, suppose the quality was not important. In that case, I could write 30 pages within the same period, so I would have created even more time. It is essential to understand the concept of value regarding whatever you do because if the action is not valuable, it is wasteful, which means you are destroying and reducing time.

So, the faster you complete valuable actions that have the highest impact on your goal, the more time you will create. And the more time you create, the fewer trade-offs you will need to make.

To help you create time, you will first need to measure where you spend your time and how long you spend it. You can do this for one day, but it is better to record it for at least a week, to better assess where your time goes and how you can improve it. Once you do that, you should still monitor your time daily, so you can do a review once a month and see what else you can do to create time. This is in line with the Japanese method of *kaizen*, which relates to continuous improvement.

Always try to improve so you can create time and value. What I have also found is that by recording the time I spend on each activity and putting a time goal for completion, I automatically do it faster, because not only am I more aware and want to do the action faster, but I also overcome Parkinson's law, which says the amount of work expands to fill the time available for its completion.

So, the more time you think you have, the longer it will take you to complete the task. Personally, I have tried many times to escape from measuring my activities, but I quickly realized my productivity was always reducing, so I always record the time I spend daily on each activity to make sure I am always aware of time.

In order to create time, you can follow the steps below:

1. List the main activities you do each day and categorize them based on your goal categories, plus an extra category: daily tasks. Each activity should also have a target time, as we defined earlier in our book

2. Record the time spent on each activity.

3. Review each activity and answer the following questions in the following order. (You do not want to delegate or improve an activity if you do not need to.)

   - Can it be eliminated, or can you just say no? Does it impact your goal?
   - Can it be delegated? Do you need to do it?
   - Can you do it faster?
   - Is the time you spend on each activity enough to reach your goal?
   - Is your time balanced?

4. Based on your responses, adjust the time you spent on each activity

Let's look at an example.

Daily Tasks

   - Grocery (**Target time**: 1 hour; **Actual time spent**: 2 hours)
   - Watch TV (**Target time**: 1 hour; **Actual time spent**: 3 hours)
   - Food preparation and eating (**Target time**: 1 hour; **Actual time spent**: 2 hours)
   - Breaks (**Target time**: 2 hours; **Actual time spent**: 1 hour)

Financial/Business

   - Create my own business (**Target time**: 2 hours; **Actual time spent**: 0 hours)
   - Working on a client project (**Target time**: 8 hours; **Actual time spent**: 10 hours)

Health/Fitness

   - Exercise (Target time: 1 hour; Actual time spent: 1 hour)
   - Meditation (**Target time**: 1 hour; **Actual time spent**: 1 hour)

Relationships

   - Spend time with family (**Target time**: 3 hours; **Actual time spent**: 1 hour)

Self-Development

- Read a book (**Target time**: 1 hour; **Actual time spent**: 0 hours)

By looking at the activities and evaluating the target and actual time spent, you can make changes to create time. For example:

Daily Tasks

- By eliminating watching TV and ordering my groceries online, I could save four and a half hours.

Financial/Business

- I need to increase the time I am working on my business, so I need to increase it to three hours per day. This is because I realized I am not spending time on this, and now I am behind in my plan.
- By working more efficiently on my client project, I can save another two hours per day.

Health/Fitness

- No change

Relationships

- I am not spending enough time with my family, so I need to increase this by two hours.

Self-Development

- I am not spending any time reading a book. I need to review the "Act Without Thinking" chapter of this book and start reading for 30 minutes daily.

You can also do it at a high level by thinking about which activities you spent most of your time doing and seeing how you can change these activities to take less time. But these are high levels, so you will not be able to maximize every second. The high-level analysis follows the Pareto rule of 80/20, which says that, on average, 80 percent of the consequences come from 20 percent of the causes. For example, if you sleep nine hours and work for ten, these two activities contribute to almost 80 percent of your time. So, by reducing these activities or being more productive, you can reduce the time you spend doing these and the remaining time to focus on actions that can help you reach your goals.

For example, suppose you can improve your quality of sleep. In that case, you can potentially reduce the number of hours you sleep. If you can automate, eliminate, or delegate any activities you do at your work, you can also save time doing the actions that can have a direct impact on your goal.

However, remember what we discussed in the Restore Energy chapter – that you need to have breaks and work patterns to maximize your productivity. You can start with 50 minutes of work and a ten-minute break and then adjust according to your needs. Make sure that for those 50 minutes, you are fully focused, with no distractions from other people, mobile phones, notifications, etc. Just be on "airplane mode" because if you are interrupted, it can take up to 25 minutes to achieve the same level of focus.

Also, ensure you are not multi-tasking and instead focusing only on the activity you are performing, as it can potentially cost you 40 percent of your productivity.

However, you can still do activity stacking, combining two activities to save you time, like listening to an audiobook while walking.

Finally, you must ensure that the time you have created is used properly. There is no point in creating time when you spend it doing something that is not valuable or does not help you achieve your goal.

> **Therefore, make sure you complete the activities that impact your goal first before you do anything else.**

Assess what you need to complete first based on the impact and importance of the task before you do the next task and try to stack rank all tasks. Stack ranking means listing all of your daily tasks in order of priority and only moving to the next task after you complete the first one. However, suppose a task cannot be completed because you need to wait for something else. In that case, you move to the next task, and you return when you receive the information that will enable you to complete the first one.

Focusing on the most important tasks first is necessary because your energy levels will decrease as the day progresses. You need to ensure you are spending your high energy on the actions that will bring you closer to your goal.

However, to be even more productive, get your mind into a state of flow, and be more creative or efficient, you need to complete your tasks based on the allocated time for each goal or activity. So, your tasks need to be on your priority list for each goal instead of completing the tasks across different goals. As we have explained, when you multi-tasking, this will decrease your productivity significantly.

We can explain the concept using the following example. Suppose you had the following goals and tasks:

Goal 1: Write a book

Task 1: Research literature

Task 2: Write 1,000 words

Goal 2: Improve financials

>Task 3: Review spending

>Task 4: Identify improvements

Goal 3: Support family

>Task 5: Go to the supermarket

>Task 6: Cook meal

The first thing we do is write the tasks in order of priority for each goal, so we do not have to think about which task we should do next. The next thing we need to do is to plan when we should complete those tasks. What I wanted to emphasize before is that you should allocate, let's say, one hour for each goal and do the tasks on each goal instead of mixing them. If you try to do Task 1, then Task 3 and Task 5, you will take more time because you are making your brain work harder, as you will have to jump through different concepts and skills. That can drain your energy, which means you will get tired faster.

Also, this will prevent your mind from going into a state of flow, which comes when you concentrate on one area. It works similarly to the way athletes practice before the race: if you go straight to the race without a warm-up, you will not be able to perform as well as if you did a proper warm-up. You need to activate your body first and warm all your muscles so they can perform better. Similarly, your mind needs to focus on one area, skill, or concept for some time to work more efficiently. You can easily try to test this concept and see how your performance improves or deteriorates.

10.
Maximize Resources

*"Start where you are with what you have,
knowing that what you have is plenty enough."*
Booker T. Washington

We often give ourselves excuses that we cannot achieve what we want because we do not have the resources. Even though it is true that you need resources to perform certain actions, it is also true that you can be *resourceful* and achieve what you want with limited resources. Choose to think that you do not need resources; you just need to be resourceful, and you will find the way. When you are resourceful, you can maximize your existing resources and find ways to create new ones. When you maximize your resources and find new ones, you do not have to make sacrifices and can achieve what you want. So next time you think you cannot do it, just say "How can I do it?" and you will find the way.

For example, finding people who have already achieved what you want and getting advice from them, can save time and money, giving you enough time to do the things you were doing before. You can use your network, find mentors, watch videos online, read books, and attend training courses, and in those ways, identify what actions you need to take to reach your goal.

Also, you can learn from other people's mistakes, so you can be educated and know what you need to avoid or where to be cautious on your journey to success. Make sure you also read and learn about why other people have failed and what they have done to overcome their failures. You can be more conscious of things and potentially avoid such failures in the future.

All this information is available to you, and you can start now. You do not have to wait for the perfect moment; the perfect second is now. A Chinese proverb says, **"The best time to plant a tree was 20 years ago. The second-best time is now."**

Take, for example, the company Tough Mudder. Will Dean started it with only $7,000 in savings and now has more than $100 million in revenue by pre-selling registrations to races. Same with Shutterstock: Jon Oringer started with 30,000 photos from his personal photo library, and now the company is worth billions of dollars.

Also, if you are thinking of building a new business or product, before you start, research what is already available in the market and how other companies have become successful. Use the resources you can find so you will not have to start from scratch. However, remember that knowledge is like a fire, and only if you use it is it useful. When you learn something, try to apply it to see how the new knowledge can help you reach your goals.

Another way you can maximize your resources is by empowering others and delegating your work, so you can focus on the things that have a higher impact. Delegating will give you more time to focus on the things that matter most so that you can add value. According to a 2018 article from *Harvard Business Review,* empowering leadership can motivate employees. So, if someone else can do it for you, and it will also motivate them, then why spend time doing it yourself?

There are always cost implications by doing that. Still, your time is precious, and you need to ensure every second counts. Try to do the things that you must do, instead of the things that you should or could do. Try to automate any activities that must be done, but you do not need to have a person do them.

Finally, you can maximise your resources by building a strong team. Having people to support you can save you a lot of time because they can bring new ideas. You will have the collective brainpower, so you can solve problems faster, increase motivation, learn faster, and have someone to cover the work.

"The whole is greater than its parts."

Aristotle

This quote is so true, and you can see that by looking at your own life and finding examples where a conversation with someone sparked in the brain thoughts that helped you solve a problem or improve something in your personal or professional life. There is also an African proverb that says, "If you want to go fast, go alone; but if you want to go far, go together."

Of course, building a team is not easy, but you can follow the research, which was published by the *New York Times Magazine*, that reported that in order to build the best team, you need to make sure members listen to each other and are sensitive to feelings and needs.

11.
Train Your Brain

Train your brain, and get there faster. When you train your brain, you will be able to perform better, which means you will not need to sacrifice your time in order to achieve what you want.

The prefrontal cortex is responsible for the executive functions of the brain, such as reasoning, creativity, problem-solving, etc. It is also responsible for cognitive control and goal-directed behaviour. Evidence has shown that performing certain exercises can develop the prefrontal cortex and enhance those executive functions. In that way, you can arrive at your goal faster. According to Moffit et al., executive functions can also predict achievement, health, and wealth. Also, in a 2006 publication by Ericsson, the improvement of executive function depends on the amount of time you spend practicing but needs to be continually challenged to go beyond one's comfort zone or current level of competence. Therefore, next time you find a challenging task, think the **challenge is growth**, and keep going.

In addition, based on a 1986 publication by Trulson, executive function improvements are also based on how an activity is presented and conducted. This is why we will sometimes believe and do something if it comes from a person we trust and is more self-confident than someone who is afraid to speak or is not confident in what he or she says.

I have found that if I intend to do something, I can learn and perform better. I did some further research and, based on a 1957 article published in the *Journal of General Psychology*, came to realize that incidental learning is less efficient than intentional learning. So next time you try to learn or do something, think that you do it because you want to learn, grow, and develop instead of doing it just because someone else told you so. This will also act as your motivation because it will give you autonomy, which, according to Pink, acts as your motivating factor.

So how can you train your brain and develop your executive functions to perform better? Below are some things that you can do:

Visualization: Visualization techniques are often used by athletes to improve their performance. When you visualize, you generate alpha waves, which increase your relaxation and focus. According to neuroscientists, the brain creates the same neural pathways when you do something or just visualize it. Also, the more vivid the visualization, the stronger the connections of the neural pathways.

Olympic gold medallist Sally Gunnell spends hours and hours visualizing each race, which she credits as contributing to her success. Same for fellow Olympic gold medallist Michael Phelps, who has used visualization techniques since he was young to stay focused and confident. So, why don't you try it yourself and see if it works?

According to a 2013 research paper by the *International Coach Academy*, if you visualize a solution to a problem, you will be able to solve the problem more easily, as it activates the cognitive circuits, which relate to the working memory. Also, if you visualize your goals, the brain will eventually believe you have achieved them, increasing your confidence. According to a May 2020 article by *Healthline*, visualization also helps create new pathways through a process called neuroplasticity, which can associate optimism and positive feelings with the goal you want to achieve.

Even more interesting is an article published by *National Geographic* in December 2010. It explains that, according to new research, if you imagine eating a specific food, it reduces your interest in that food. So, not only can you use visualization to increase your performance, but you can also use it to control the food you eat.

I use visualization techniques all the time. I am visualizing my basketball game to improve my performance and my game. I am visualizing my dance moves by dancing with an imaginary partner (this way, I can practice my new moves and become better at these even without physically dancing). I am also using visualization techniques to relax, by either doing a body scan to relax all the parts of my body or by visualizing I am walking in a favourite place, like the small streets of St Germain in Paris. I also visualize my vision board to increase my confidence and belief that I can achieve anything I want. There are so many applications, and you can decide what suits you best.

A simple mindbodism visualization technique is as follows:

1. Sit or lie down to get comfortable.

2. Close your eyes and take three deep breaths, so you can start relaxing and clearing your mind. Make sure all of your vertebrae are aligned, so your back is straight.

3. Feel that you are safe, protected and that you can open your imagination.

4. To complete a goal visualization, pick a goal and, with your five senses, see how it feels when you achieve your goal.

5. To complete a body scan visualization, imagine a light starting slowly on top of your head and going down through each part of your body. Feel the light as it warms you, releases tension, and heals your body, all the way down to your toes.

6. To complete a place visualization – to release stress, make you happy, and help you focus on positive thoughts – imagine you are in your favourite place on Earth and walk down the streets of that place and, with your five senses, observe everything around you.

7. When you feel ready, you can slowly open your eyes, do a light stretch, and be grateful for this positive feeling.

Positive thinking: Focusing on positive thinking and rejecting any negative thoughts, can ensure that the prefrontal cortex remains engaged. Otherwise, the amygdala can be activated, which will limit the prefrontal cortex activities. When you think positively, you feel happier and more optimistic, which decreases cortisol (your stress hormone), and the brain produces serotonin (your mood stabilizer).

Also, according to author and science journalist Daniel Goleman, positive thinking can enhance creative thinking and your mental functions, such as processing things faster. On the contrary, according to Peter Marien, an expert on neurolinguistics and neuropsychology, negative thoughts reduce activity in the cerebellum, which relates to balance, working relationships, and speed of thought. Similarly, Robert Sapolsky, a neuro-endocrinology researcher, explains that even 30 minutes of negative speech will cause the neuron cells – located in the hippocampus, which relates to problem-solving – to begin to die. Therefore, practicing positive thinking can improve your performance, leading to doing things faster and not sacrificing your time.

These are some techniques I use to always stay positive:

If something bad happens, or if I fail at something, I say, "**Life will give you what you need and not what you want.**" I will try to reflect and learn from this bad experience, take the related negative energy, and transform it into something positive. When I could not find anywhere to play basketball for two months, I created my own company and rented a court to be able to play basketball. A few years later, anyone can join one of these sessions.

I also say, "**Failure is a step to success.**" And then again, I try to improve and learn from my mistakes continuously.

If someone tries to behave badly toward me, I say, "**When you under-stand, you forgive.**" I remember that not everyone is privileged to have good education or loving childhood, and if you truly pay attention and understand why people behave in a certain way, you will forgive. And remember, no one is perfect.

When something bad happens, I tend to change the narrative so it will not sound as bad. For example, if someone says something hurtful, I will try not to put my ego first and magnify the situation by thinking that person does not respect me or does not care about me. Instead, I will change the narrative to this person being unable to understand in that moment or they are unable to think and speak properly.

Change your language; move from negative self-talk to positive self-talk. Say "How can I do it?" instead of "I cannot do it." Say, "I'll make it work," instead of saying, "It will not work." Say "It is possible" instead of "It is impossible". Say "I'll learn the skill" instead of "I do not have the skill." Say, "I'll find a way," instead of "It is too difficult."

When I am trying not to have negative thoughts, I try to smile and think something positive. Smiling makes me focus on being positive and melts any negative emotions.

The days I exercise, eat healthily, and take control of my day by deciding what to do and not to do, always help me keep a positive attitude and think positively throughout the day.

Moderate-intensity exercise is also recommended to enhance your cognitive functions. These exercises will raise your heart rate, make you breathe faster, and feel warmer. One practical way to check if you are doing moderate exercise is to see if you can talk but not sing.

Low-intensity exercise has a smaller impact but is still beneficial. High-intensity workouts can have the opposite effect if you exceed your limit. In an article published in July 2019 by *Behaviour Sciences*, activation changes in the prefrontal cortex are higher after moderate-intensity exercise compared to high-intensity. Also, according to a 2014 article by Harvard Health Publishing, if you exercise regularly, your brain will change to improve memory and thinking skills, as it stimulates the release of growth chemicals (which affect the health of brain cells and the growth of new blood vessels in the brain). A 2020 article by *Harvard Health Publishing* explains that exercising, reduces stress hormones like cortisol and epinephrine, as endorphins are produced. Endorphins are chemicals in the brain that act as natural painkillers.

Below you can find some moderate-intensity exercises you can do:

1. Dancing
2. Riding a bike
3. Playing tennis
4. Brisk walking
5. Jogging
6. Swimming

Gratitude enhances positive emotions, which also activate the prefrontal cortex. According to Emily Fletcher, an expert in meditation high performance, when we practice gratitude, our brain releases dopamine and serotonin, which are the neurotransmitters responsible for making us feel good. When you show gratitude, you acknowledge the good things in life. Also, gratitude is associated with happiness, which you can see from your own experience. Therefore, practicing gratitude will make us feel happier, and that, in turn, will help us be more productive.

Below you can find some mindbodism techniques on how to practice gratitude:

1. When you wake up in the morning and before you go to bed, say **five things you are grateful for.** When you say thank you, you need to have your eyes closed and your palms together and resting on your chest so that your hands are touching your heart.

When you say thank you, also explain why. For example, you can be thankful for your health because you can complete the things you want to do. You can be grateful for your family because they are with you to support you. You can be thankful for the sun because it makes you happy and keeps you warm. You can be grateful for the lunch you ate because it was nourishing and tasted great.

Do not limit yourself by only practicing gratitude during the day and at night. When you find yourself stressed, disappointed, or having negative thoughts, be grateful for what you have, and smile when you finish each sentence. Keeping a journal can also be helpful because you can always go back and remember all the things you have been grateful. The more positive memories, the greater you will feel.

2. **Say thank you to at least one person daily.** You can thank your wife for cooking dinner, you can thank your husband for giving you flowers, or you can thank a colleague for helping you complete a task.

3. **Complete a gratitude meditation.** You can find a gratitude meditation at mindbodism.com or look online to find one that connects better with you.

4. **Be thankful for a challenge or difficult situation you have overcome.** Remember that when something bad happens, something good will follow in the future.

5. **Create your own gratitude prayer,** or you can use the one from mindbodism below. When you say thank you, you need to have your eyes closed, your palms touching together and resting on your chest, and your hands touching your heart.

Thank you for the precious life you have given me. I am grateful for every second I spend in my life, and I promise I will not waste a moment. Thank you for your love, kindness, empathy, forgiveness, and hope for a better future. Thank you for keeping me, my family, and my friends safe and protected under your wings. Thank you for the body, mind, and spirit you have given me to allow me to connect with others in so many ways and awaken my spirit. Thank you for the challenges you bring to my life, and for the strength and intelligence, you give me to overcome them so they can help me grow. Thank you for showing me how to appreciate and value every second and for helping me achieve my purpose in life. Thank you for everything. Namaste.

6. **Learn something new.** According to an article published in February 2015 by *Harvard Health Publishing*, when we practice a new and challenging activity, doing so may build and maintain cognitive skills because our brains can learn and grow – a process called brain plasticity. Also, according to an earlier article published in December 2015, challenging your brain may help keep your thinking skills sharp. By learning something new, you exercise your brain, which helps improve cognitive functions such as concentration and problem-solving. Therefore, by learning something new, you will also be able to perform better, so you won't have to sacrifice your time.

However, to maximize the benefit of learning something new, you need to try to perform an activity, which is challenging – this is the reason why you choose something new. A good example is starting to learn a new dance. Initially, when I started learning salsa, I did not know how to coordinate moving my left foot with moving my right. After years of practice, I was not only able to learn how to dance but also how to be a performer and choreographer. Also, when you choose complex activities, you can exercise more of your brain and work on problem-solving.

Here are some ways to start learning:

- Learn how to dance, or learn a new dance
- Learn a new sport
- Learn how to paint
- Learn to play a musical instrument
- Write a book
- Learn a new language
- Read a new book

7. **Focus on breathwork**. In an article published in March 2015 by the *National Library of Medicine*, researchers found that a simple breathing practice can help improve cognitive processes. The study participants were tested on mental math and working memory, and they performed significantly better after six weeks of intervention. So, as you practice your breathing – and you can perform better – you will not have to sacrifice your time to do the things you used to do.

The relationship between breathing and mind was actually known way before as Yogi Swatarama, fifteenth and sixteenth century yogic sage in India, wrote: "When the breath wanders, the mind is unsteady. But when the breath is calmed, the mind too will be still."

Below are the main types of breathing you can follow:

1. **Ratio breathing**. In this type of breathing, you change the ratio of inhaling and exhaling. So, for example, if you use a one to two ratio, you need to breathe for two seconds and exhale for four seconds – or the opposite, and inhale for ten seconds and exhale for five. According to an article published in August 2014 from *Applied Psychophysiology,* when you inhale, you activate the sympathetic

nervous system, which is made of neural circuits that cause your heart rate and attention to increase. This is the "fight or flight" response that your body activates when it senses a threat.

On the other hand, when you exhale, you activate the parasympathetic team, which activates when you feel relaxed and safe. Then your heart rate slows downs, and you become calmer.

So, if you want to relax, be calm, and release stress, exhale more than you inhale, and if you want to be focused, alert, and awake, inhale more than you exhale.

A simple breathing practice you can do is to just sit in a comfortable position or stand straight up, and breathe in for three seconds, hold for four seconds, breathe out for six seconds, and hold for three seconds.

If you want to feel more alert, breathe in for six seconds, hold for three, breath out for three seconds, and hold for four.

2. **Nostril breathing.** When you practice nostril breathing, you block one nostril with your finger, exerting pressure to the side, and then you inhale and exhale from the other nostril. And then you switch. You can also block one nostril inhale from the other, then block the other and exhale from the nostril that is open. You can also alternate nostrils with every full breath.

According to a November 2018 article from the *Journal of Neuroscience*, breathing through the nose has been found to enhance recognition memory.

12.
Use the Two Superpowers

If you can imagine it, you can create it, and if you can create it, you can make it into reality, and if you can make it into reality, you can achieve your goal.

The two superpowers are IMAGINATION and CREATIVITY. Imagination is a mental picture of something not present, and creativity is the ability to create something using imagination. These are superpowers because you can generate new ideas and solve problems in unique ways, which can act as a magic key to unlocking any problem you might have. This can help you do things faster, saving time, so you don't have to make sacrifices.

Many examples of successful people have used their imagination and creativity to produce something great. Thomas Edison produced 1000 patents. Isaac Newton discovered the laws of gravity and motion. Albert Einstein developed the theory of special and general relativity. Leonardo da Vinci created the Mona Lisa and conceptually invented the scissors, the parachute, the helicopter, and more.

"Imagination is more important than knowledge.
For knowledge is limited, whereas imagination embraces the
entire world, stimulating progress and giving birth to evolution."
Albert Einstein

When you use your imagination, you use the power to form mental images of something you have never experienced before or something that is not present. Using your imagination, you can also simulate events in your mind and observe potential outcomes without actually performing the task.

Imagination is a superpower because you can also use it while you sleep. There are many examples in the past when people got inspired by a dream and created something important. For example, Otto Lowei dreamed of an experiment on nerve impulses that made him wake up and perform the experiment, which later earned him the Nobel Prize. Dmitri Mendeleev, who discovered the periodic table, first dreamed about a table in which all the elements fell in place. Elias Howe, who discovered the sewing machine needle, first had dreamed of warriors carrying spears that were pierced near the head. When he woke up, he created the model.

According to an article published in January 2019 by Andrey Vyshedskiy, it seems that the mind's internal imagery while awake is from the front end of the brain and conducted by the lateral prefrontal cortex, while vivid dreaming is driven from the back of the brain posterior cortex, and the lateral prefrontal cortex is inactive. However, what is interesting is that you can produce the same mental image both when you are awake or sleeping.

Also, Mark Jung-Beeman found that people just before having a eureka moment, there is a burst of high-frequency gamma-band neural activity that is produced. Furthermore, according to Earl K. Miller, your conscious mind often limits your choices based on previous experiences or knowledge. However, when you tap into your unconscious mind without thinking about the problem you want to solve, you can generate ideas and solutions. Creativity, on the other hand, uses imagination in order to create.

> *"Creativity is intelligence having fun."*
> Albert Einstein

When you are creative, you can see the world in new ways; find patterns that are not obvious; make connections between events, concepts, and usages that seem unrelated; and solve problems in creative ways. Once you can do that, you can do things more quickly, so you will not have to make sacrifices.

According to a 2004 article by the *Creativity Research Journal*, creativity can be learned. However, according to a study that George Land completed in 1968, being non-creative is learned because as we grow, it seems we become less creative.

Also, a study published in January 2020 by Dana Foundation showed that highly creative people have stronger functional connections between the default network, the executive control network, and the switching that occurs between the two. A Default network is a group of brain regions that seems to have higher activity when we are awake but not while exercising our brain, while the executive control network shows activation during cognitively – and emotionally – challenging activities. The good news is that we can become more creative, and, according to Mobley, we need to unlearn rather than learn the process, so we can think outside of the box.

Below are some ways that you can enhance your imagination and creativity:

1. **Let your mind wander.** Taking a walk, listening to music without lyrics, or even just daydreaming, doing nothing, and letting your mind wander, can enhance your creativity, as the mind does not have to think. This is also a very important practice in mind-bodism, in which you can tap into your unconscious mind, connect with the universe, and open your brain funnel so that ideas can flow in your mind.

   I have to say that many ideas came to me using this practice. From starting a new business to reaching out to someone, I have not seen for years, everything was somehow connected to help me achieve my goal. You can find out more at www.mindbodism.com

2. **Change your surroundings.** Switch items on your desk, or enhance your surrounding with blue colour. According to Robert Epstein, a psychologist at the American Institute of Behavioural Research, even minimal changes can affect your creativity.

3. **Write or draw.** When you have an idea or want to draw something, just do it – capturing this can boost your creativity. Girija Kaimal, a researcher in art therapy, states that anything that engages your creative mind and makes connections between unrelated things helps.

4. **Think about a problem and go crazy.** See how you can solve the problem by suggesting solutions that might seem insane, like solving the problem of water on Earth by extracting water from planet Mars. Also, according to Caneel Joyce, using constraints when solving a problem can help generate ideas you cannot afford or ideas with which you need other people to help you.

5. **Listen to music.** Einstein credited his creativity to listening to Mozart

6. **Be around creative people.** According to Mobley Matrix, a former director of the IBM Executive School, the fastest way to become creative is to hang out with creative people. This is a fundamental concept because it has many applications, as seen in other research. For example, being around rich people increases your likelihood of becoming rich. You can increase the likelihood of starting your own business if you are around entrepreneurs. You can be healthier and more fit if you are around people that exercise and eat healthily.

7. **Keep creating.** A lot of people are sensitive to criticism, so some people will stop creating if they get bad feedback. However, you should not be one of them. Keep creating, keep evolving your ideas, and continue making new connections, and soon you will realize your creativity has been enhanced. Dyson created 5,126 prototypes before he completed the first Dyson vacuum cleaner.

13.
Predict Your Future

No one can predict your future as accurately as you can.

The reason you need to predict your future is so that you do not have to make sacrifices. Once you can predict the future, you can make faster decisions, avoid mistakes, and grow faster. But how is it possible to predict your future when it is so uncertain, when there are so many variables and when change happens so quickly?

There is a way to predict your future, in some way, without using a crystal ball. Begin by applying the following techniques:

1. **Visualize the future.** If you visualize your future in a lot of detail and believe in it, the future will unfold as you imagined it. We have shown throughout the book techniques that will empower you to do that.

2. **1+1=2.** We have also explained the concept of 1+1=2, where your need to find the actions that impact your goal. Once you learn what those actions are, then you will know that if you fail to do these actions, you will not achieve your goal.

   For example, if I want to be fit, and I know I need to eat healthily and exercise, if I do the opposite, I will not be able to reach the goal. So, you can predict how the future will unfold based on the actions you take. Similarly, if you want to become a millionaire, and you do not dedicate any time to completing the steps that will help you reach that goal, then I can predict that you will never become one. Even buying a lottery ticket is an action toward becoming a millionaire, but if you do not do anything at all, you will never reach that goal. Try to use as much data as you can to be able to make better predictions.

3. **Play the game in your head.** This means trying to visualize the impact of each action you will take to achieve your goals before actually taking the action. Apply what-if scenarios, and imagine the other possible ways you can achieve the same goal. Additionally, you need to be proactive and prepare for things that might happen in the future before they happen. In that way, you will be able to prevent failures, as you will have already seen the scenario in your mind.

   It is similar to what some great chess players do: visualize the board of chess – the different moves and combinations in their head – so they can predict the opponent's next moves and how they will respond to those moves. For example, signing up for health insurance can protect me from spending a huge amount of money if something goes wrong with my health. After playing the scenario of "what if I become ill in the future?" I was proactive and bought health insurance.

4. **Value creation.** This is very important because not only can it indicate if you will succeed or not, but it can make you focus on the important things and have a bigger impact on your goal.

   Value is something that you – the customers, the investors, and the stakeholders – find useful because it can provide benefits such as increasing revenue or profitability in the business, improving your health, enhancing your emotional state, etc. It is something you want, and you usually are willing to pay for it.

   For example, if we are developing a product but there is no value or benefit to the customers, then we can predict that this product will most likely fail. Before you do something, you need to understand who will receive the benefit and if they are willing to pay for it. Willingness to pay is an important factor because many people want more, but if they are not willing to pay, it is not that important.

So, if the customer wants a bigger seat on an airplane, but is not willing to pay more, then we can understand that cost is more important to the customer than space. However, it also depends on the business model because sometimes the customer is unwilling to pay, but you receive money from other means like affiliate sales, advertising, etc.

To summarise:

1. **Change the view of the world.** You will not sacrifice if you love what you are doing.

2. **Create a plan,** which will save you time, as it shows you what you need to do and in which order you need to do things, to reach your goal. A good plan can enhance your belief that you can succeed and prevent you from failing.

3. **Create time; every second counts.** Treat time as gold and measure it, analyze it and optimize it, so you can create more time to do the things you want. Also, prioritize and stack-rank your activities, and avoid multitasking to complete tasks more quickly and effectively.

4. **Maximize the resources and get there faster.** Use different resources to acquire knowledge, and learn from previous failures so you can save time by avoiding the same mistakes. Also, try to delegate, empower, and build a strong team to save you time and reach your goal faster.

5. **Train your brain.** Exercise your brain to enhance your prefrontal cortex, which is responsible for the brain's cognitive functions, so you can do things faster and save time.

6. **Use the two superpowers.** Use imagination and creativity to become resourceful and solve faster problems by creating new solutions in unique ways.

7. **Predict the future.** Apply visualization of the future, understand the 1+1=2 actions impacting your goal, play the game in your head by visualizing future scenarios and actions that you will take in the future, and understand value creation.

PART 4:

HOW TO FIND THE PATH
YOU NEED TO FOLLOW

14.
Follow Your Life's Purpose

Sometimes you find your path; sometimes it finds you.

Max Brooks

You now have the toolset to achieve anything you want in life, but it is also essential to discuss your life path. Many people set goals and can achieve them, but they still feel as if something is missing from their life. They feel that they have not yet found their purpose in life – the reason for their existence – and that makes them incomplete, no matter what they achieve.

Know that from the time you are born until the day you die, you are fulfilling a purpose in this life. It is there even if you do not know what that purpose is. We are all connected in some way, and as we are connected, we impact each other's lives. We are impacting people; become aware of how you do so in your daily life. You can say something to someone that can make him feel good or bad, and that person can take an action that is good or bad. We are impacting animals – you can kill an insect or care for a dog. And we are impacting nature – we can water a flower, and it can blossom, or we can step on it and let it die.

Therefore, even if you cannot articulate, or do not know, your purpose in life, you should know that your life is meaningful because you are impacting the world around you. So do not stress yourself trying to find it; you are already living your life's purpose, even if you do not know it yet. When you have doubts, remember this quote:

There are two ways to live your life. One is as though nothing is a miracle. The other is as though everything is a miracle.

Albert Einstein

Also, you need to know that when you set goals, even if none of them is your life's purpose, they can lead you to the path you need to follow to find it, and one day, one of those goals can become your life purpose.

Remember, your life purpose can change, so focus on your goals, and you will find your purpose. There will be choices you will need to make. However, that will significantly change your life in one second. It can be starting a new relationship, quitting your old job and starting a new one, creating your own business – so many choices. How do you know which choices to make, and if you make these choices, how do you know which are the right ones for you? Should these be based on intuition or logic?

15.
Follow Your Logic, Follow Your Intuition

When intuition and logic agree,
the choice you make is the right one.

But when intuition and logic do not agree, the choice you make is the right one as well. Therefore, the only thing you need to do is make a choice and act on it. Do not worry about whether or not your choice was the right one, because it always is.

Many people face the dilemma of following logic or their intuition and are often unable to choose. They want to set a goal, live a certain way, follow a path, or take action, but they cannot decide what to do or which choice to trust. Should they choose based on their logic or their intuition?

Logic is when you use something you have learned to come up with a decision, like solving a math equation. Intuition uses abstract information you have received to make a decision, like when you get a hunch to build a company.

Many successful people have chosen to follow their intuitions. Steve Jobs quit college after one semester and went backpacking through India. After coming back, he started Apple. He said, "Have the courage to follow your heart and intuition. They somehow know what you truly want to become."

Oprah Winfrey followed her instincts and, when they told her she was unfit for television news, she did not quit. She said, "Follow your instincts. That's where true wisdom manifests itself."

Bill Gates dropped out of Harvard to build a company that later became Microsoft, and he said, "Often you have just to decide on your intuition."

Many successful people follow their intuitions because over time they become less risk-averse, are more open, and can make decisions faster. In that way, they are not afraid to fail and start again until they succeed.

But what happens to our brain? According to an article published in May 2018 by the *World Economic Forum*, the brain is like a machine, trying to predict the outcome by comparing sensory information and experiences against stored knowledge and memories of previous experiences. When the prediction is not accurate, it adjusts the cognitive models. However, this happens automatically and subconsciously, so you are unaware of that. So, someone will think that following intuition is what you should do, but that is not always true.

There are examples where people used their intuitions and lost a fortune, such as George Soros when he speculated in Russian securities and bet on technology stocks. Also, for those who have conducted interviews, you might have had a good hunch to hire someone but eventually found that person was unsuitable for the job. This is because intuition also includes your cultural and emotional biases.

So, should we go with logic or intuition? Let's take the following example. Which option would you choose?

You want to become a millionaire and a writer. You can use your logic and say that only a very small percentage of millionaires are writers, so you can choose to maybe become a business owner instead. However, you can also decide to become a writer because you have a big passion for writing – perhaps you have already thought of a book you want to write.

The other option is to do both. You can become a successful business owner first and then become a writer or work on both goals simultaneously by dedicating time to doing both daily. Which one is the correct option?

The answer is that it does not matter; the only thing that matters is having a goal and dedicating your time to doing the actions that impact your goal daily.

Focus on this second. You make a choice; you are responsible for your destiny. Even if you fail, if you are persistent, you will try different things, and you will succeed. Maybe sometimes you use your logic, sometimes you use your intuition, or sometimes you use both. The important thing is to try things out and see what is working for you. Your life can change within one second, so you will never know which choice was better, and that is why you should never have regrets. Something can happen, and you can die in one second.

Failure is the process of success, so do not waste your time trying to decide which option to choose because you will never know. You might select something, which has a higher probability of success and fail. You might select something, which has a lower likelihood of success and become successful. For example, the probability of broke people becoming millionaires is very low – but some do it.

If you still fear of trying something new, choose to think differently. If you have an idea and decide not to do anything about it, know that the alternative is to go back to your comfort zone and waste your time doing things that do not have value and do not grow you. The new experiences you collect each day will be used in the future, even if now you cannot see the connection.

Steve Jobs took a calligraphy class, which led him to the inspiration for Apple's calligraphy. He said, "**Again, you can't connect the dots looking forward; you can only connect them looking backwards. So, you have to trust that the dots will somehow connect in your future. You have to trust in something: your gut, destiny, life, karma, whatever. This approach has never let me down, and it has made all the difference in my life.**"

If you usually operate with logic and you want to use your intuition more, these are some things you need to consider.

1. **Check how you are feeling.** You need to remember that if something bad has happened to you or you feel upset, it is more difficult to tap into your intuition. And even if you think it is your intuition, it may be your emotionally thinking. According to a study conducted in 2017 at Basel University, anxious participants showed decreased intuitive performance against those with positive or neutral moods. This is the reason why we sometimes say we will say "sleep on it" when we have to make an important decision or before we reply to an e-mail from someone who has offended us. It is better to take a few hours to calm down to avoid sending an inappropriate response. So, make sure you are calm before you make a gut decision. Someone once said, **"If you are patient in one moment of anger, you will escape a hundred days of sorrow."**

2. **Increase your interoceptive awareness.** An interoception occurs when you become aware of your body signals. For example, the brain does not think you are hungry, but instead, it receives a signal from the stomach that says it needs food – your stomach may even growl. According to Joel Pearson, a professor of cognitive neuroscience, when you have an interoception, you are more likely to sense when you have a gut feeling. The more you cultivate somatic awareness, the more sensitive you become. Try to pay attention to any physical feeling you get when you try to make a decision. You can enhance your interoception with focused attention mindfulness, in which you try to focus on a particular aspect of your body, such as breathing, and observe the sensations as they pass through, without judging or engaging with them.

3. **Check if the situation or experience is new.** If the situation or experience is new, it is better to rely on logic. In an article published in April 2015 by *Harvard Business Review*, researchers say it takes around ten years of domain-specific expertise to develop accurate intuitive judgments, and only if you repeat and receive feedback frequently. This is why when you practice flow state, and you see your intuition is working and getting positive feedback, then your intuition enhances. However, if you are an expert and you use your logic, then your intuition might be a problem. In an article published by the *Observer* in December 2016, when experienced radiologists looked at X-rays for more than 30 seconds, their decisions got worse.

4. **Make mistakes; be an explorer.** Since intuition is built by gaining experience and recognizing patterns based on the information you receive, you need to make sure you seek new experiences, learn new things, practice, and try to understand cause and effect and the relationships between how things work. That is why it is essential to understand the 1+1=2 concept we discussed earlier.

   Also, according to Janice Deakin and Stephen Cobley, researchers on expert performance in sports, high-performance figure skaters fall more often because they attempt more jumps that they have not mastered. However, this is why they are high performers.

5. **Check the type of problem.** Intuition is better used when the problem does not have clear decision rules or objective criteria. If it does, then it is better to use the data to find the potential best solution. However, most of the time, the answer is somewhere in between, where you use both intuition and analysis.

6. **Take time for yourself.** To enhance your intuition, you need to recharge and unplug. According to an October 2021 article in *Forbes*, highly intuitive people seek solitude, stop listening to others and start listening to themselves. They also take breaks, walk in nature, and seek stillness and silence.

7. **Feel more.** When you try to focus on your feelings rather than your thoughts, you will start enhancing your intuition. Focus on surrender, in which you surrender to your feelings and your inner self and resist any temptation to revert to thinking. There is also a mindbodism practice to awaken your kundalini life force energy by surrendering.

8. **Focus on breathing.** When you control your breathing, you calm your brain, and it is easier to tap into your intuition. According to a November 2017 article in *Forbes*, a neural circuit in the brainstem can be adjusted by changing the breathing rhythm. If you breathe slowly, it decreases the activity in the circuit, but when you breathe fast, it enhances it.

16.
Reflect On Your Path

"Sometimes the bad things that happen in our lives put us directly on the path to the best things that will ever happen to us."

Nicole Reed

We talked about following a path using logic or intuition, but how do you know if the path you have taken is the right one for you? To answer this question, you can use your consciousness and the feedback loop we discussed earlier. The following topics will help you identify if you are off track:

1. **Obsession**. Are you completely obsessed with something and putting all your focus and energy on that thing without paying attention to anything else? Obsession can be good, as it can create a big motivation and drive to do something. It can even create an ecstatic experience, where you lose track of time and be highly productive. However, daily obsession without breaks can lead to collapse, health issues, and broken relationships. Therefore, as you remember in the maintain momentum chapter, you need to restore your energy so you will not burn out and use some of the existing energy on your other goals to ensure you are balanced.

2. **The universe is against you**. Do you find that everything is just *wrong*? Maybe you have been fired, have health issues, just broke off a relationship, are depressed, or are not feeling well – all of these are signs that something is broken, and you need to fix it.

   This is the perfect time to change because you know that something is going wrong, and you need to use the toolset you have learned to change your life and achieve your goals. Remember, however, that you should not be blaming yourself because, in real life, we all face difficulties, make mistakes, and experience failures. As we discussed:

Failure is a process that leads to success.

Remember, do not wish for life to be easy; instead, wish for a life in which you are equipped with what you need to face any life situation.

Life will sometimes send you what you need and not what you want.

Do not ask for it to stop raining; ask for the skills you need to be able to dance in the rain.

Focus your mind on the things you can control and not what you cannot – this is also one of the secrets of happiness.

3. **You have no goals.** Maybe you have achieved your goals, or you are living your life as a drifter without any specific goals. This indicates that you are not living your life to its maximum potential. Some people may say, "I love my comfort zone; I do not want to have any goals. I have everything, so why do I need to set goals?"

    The choice is yours, but you need to make sure you are comfortable with the answers you give to the following two questions:

    1. Is there anything I want to do and have not done in this life, and how does this make me feel?

    2. Can my situation change in the future, and is there anything else I need to do today to be prepared for the future?

4. **Bad attitude.** If you find yourself not treating people with respect, not helping others, being aggressive, or not being a good person – all of these are signs that something is not right in your path, and you need to work on it. However, remember you are not a bad person, and you are not a good person; you are both good and bad. You might be good in some situations and bad in others, so you need to pay attention to your inner voice and ignore it when it tries to convince you to do something bad. Instead, pay attention to the other voice, which is there to help your reach your goal in the right way.

You are like a flower. If you feed the flower with water, it will grow. If you feed it with poison, it will die. You have the choice of what to feed the flower, as you can choose what to feed your mind, so the actions you choose can have a positive or negative impact on you and your community.

17.
Link Your Path to Happiness

"There is no way to happiness. Happiness is the path."
Buddha

You have chosen a path based on logic, intuition, or both, and you have reflected on it to see if this is the right path for you. But you still have one more question: *will I be happy if I do all these things?*

What is happiness? Happiness has many different definitions, but it always refers to an emotional state where you feel joy and satisfaction and is always related to positive emotions.

Since it is an emotional state, we can understand that it is not a permanent feeling. If some people say they have found happiness, that does not mean that it will last forever. We want to understand what is important in order to be happy and then ensure we have some goals that will reach us closer to that happiness. Also, we want to explore what actions we can take to become happy, so we can understand that we can take control of our happiness today – it only depends on us.

However, you may need to be reminded of the story of Abd-al-Rahman III. Back in the tenth century, despite having all of his material and biological needs satisfied, when, towards the end of his life, he counted the number of days of genuine happiness, the number was 14. So do not think that you will be happy if you achieve your material and biological goals. Also, according to a July 2019 article from *Neuroscience News*, happiness has no neurological basis and cannot be found in the brain tissue.

But there is a neurotransmitter named dopamine, which is a chemical substance released by neurons and associated with positive emotions and feelings, which sets in motion the neural circuits involved in motivation. Most types of rewards increase the level of dopamine in the brain. Dopamine is also called a "feel good" chemical. According to an article published in May 2018 by *Healthline*, when large amounts of dopamine are released, this motivates you to repeat a specific behaviour. Therefore, we can link dopamine with the feeling of happiness.

Then we have endorphins, which are chemicals produced by the central nervous system and pituitary gland to relieve stress and pain. They can also be produced during activities such as eating, exercise, or sex and give the feeling of being "high." According to a July 2021 article by *Harvard Health Publishing*, endorphin is the body's natural painkiller and is commonly referred to as the "pain relief" chemical. Again, since endorphins can release pain and give you positive feelings, they can also be linked to the feeling of happiness.

Also, according to an article in 2015 by *Science Direct*, endorphin is also closely linked to the release of oxytocin. Oxytocin is a hormone, often referred to as the "love hormone," because it increases during hugging and orgasm. According to an article from *Healthline*, published in August 2018, oxytocin, dopamine, and serotonin are often referred to as "happy hormones." When you are attracted to someone, your brain will release dopamine, oxytocin, and your serotonin levels will increase.

Serotonin is the key hormone responsible for your mood and feelings of well-being and happiness. According to an August 2020 article from *Healthline*, it is also referred to as a "mood stabilizer." Serotonin deficiency can result in anxiety or depression.

Since these four chemicals – dopamine, serotonin, endorphin, and oxytocin – can help you feel positive and can give the feeling of happiness, we should look at a few activities you can do to increase, boost, and produce those chemicals.

1. **Exercise:** It should come as no surprise that if you exercise regularly, you will automatically feel better. When you exercise, the body releases endorphins, so you get the "runner's high" feeling. Combine that with a cold shower, and you can also increase dopamine, the pleasure chemical that makes us feel happy. According to a March 2020 article by the *American Psychological Association,* physical activity may release dopamine and serotonin.

2. **Eat healthily:** Eating healthy food will also boost your dopamine. High protein food can help, like tyrosine and phenylalanine, which are found in high-protein food, produce dopamine. According to an article from *Nutritionist Resource* published in April 2021, dopamine-boosting foods include a lean protein such as beef, lamb, fish, and pork; avocado; bananas; cheese; nuts; beans; whole grains; and probiotic-rich food such as kefir and kimchi.

   Also, avoiding sugar and eating less saturated fat can help the flow of dopamine, as consuming too much can stop the dopamine signaling in the brain. Eating healthy also increases serotonin, which is linked to our emotions and mood. When it is released, you have feelings of satisfaction and optimism. According to an article published in August 2020 by *Healthline*, food that can increase serotonin levels includes eggs, cheese, pineapples, tofu, salmon, nuts and seeds, and turkey.

3. **Healthy relationships:** When you have healthy relationships, and a support group around you, like family and friends, as well as a sense of belonging, this can make you feel happy. When you have someone to talk to and connect with, you do not feel lonely. Also, when you have a contact like hugging, kissing or having sex, you release oxytocin, which helps you feel loved and connected. In a November 2013 article in *Psychology Today,* when you touch someone, such as giving a hug, not only does it increase oxytocin, but it

can also improve the immune system and reduce cardiovascular stress. Combine that with laughing with your close friends, and you can also release endorphin. Also, according to a June 2017 article in *Science Daily*, researchers found that laughter releases endorphins in the brain, which can boost pleasure.

4. **Massage:** You can increase your levels of dopamine, oxytocin, and serotonin levels – three essential chemicals that can help you feel happy – by getting a massage. Also, massage decreases cortisol, which is the hormone produced while stressed. According to an October 2005 article in the *International Journal of Neuroscience,* massage therapy has stress-relieving effects, as well as activating effects on various medical conditions and stressful experiences.

5. **Happy visualization**: You can visualize a happy moment from the past or create a happy memory in the future and live that moment again. Your thoughts will be focused on something positive, which can also make you feel happy, as doing this increases serotonin. According to a November 2011 article published in *Psychology Today*, remembering positive events increases serotonin. Also, it prevents serotonin decrease because you can't remember bad events at the same time as good ones.

   People who have depression normally cannot recall a positive event and just remember being depressed all the time. You can change this by shifting your focus on a positive event and letting serotonin do its magic.

6. **Sun therapy:** Spending five to ten minutes sitting in the sun and absorbing its vibrant energy can also make you feel happy, increasing your serotonin levels. According to a November 2011 article in *Psychology Today*, sunlight has similar effects to antidepressants.

7. **Listening to music.** Calming music can increase your mood, relax you, and enhance the feeling of happiness as your dopamine and oxytocin levels increase. According to an article published in February 2013 by *PsyPost*, listening to the music you love helps release more dopamine. Oxytocin levels can also be increased, as explained in an article published in September 2013 by *Frontiers in Human Neuroscience*, which will give a feeling of relaxation. Also, in a study done in August 2013 and published in *Plos One*, listening to music can help reduce cortisol, which is the "fight-or-flight" response and the body's main stress hormone.

8. **Meditation.** Meditation also increases dopamine, endorphin, and oxytocin levels, which improves focus, concentration, and the feeling of happiness. According to an article published in May 2018 by *Healthline*, meditating for an hour may result in a 64 percent increase in dopamine release. Also, according to an *Insider* article published in November 2020, you can release endorphins by meditating. Oxytocin also seems to be related to spirituality, as a study published in September 2016 by *Duke Today* revealed that participants reported a greater sense of spirituality when they received oxytocin.

9. **Sleep.** Sleep helps repair and renew all of the cells in the body, and it washes away toxins that are built during the day. Lack of sleep can reduce dopamine levels. The recommended hours of sleep for adults are between seven to nine. In an article published in March 2018 in the *Harvard Gazette*, being sleep-deprived inhibited certain parts of dopamine transmission in participants.

10. **Gratitude:** Gratitude is also linked to happiness, as it increases the release of dopamine and serotonin, as explained in an article published in September 2021 by *Positive Psychology*. Just write five things that you are grateful for each day, and you will start seeing the difference after a week.

11. **New experiences:** New experiences also release dopamine. It does not matter what experience you do; you can try a new food or take a different route to your house. The less familiar the experience, the more likely you will release dopamine. According to an article published in August 2016 by Neuron, participants activated the "pleasure centers" of the brain when a new picture was shown to them. Therefore, try to seek new experiences and monitor your happiness levels.

12. **Natural oils.** Oils from plants that enhance your sense of smell, such as lavender, bergamot, and lemon, also prompt your brain to release serotonin and dopamine. According to an article published in July 2013 by the *National Library of Medicine,* various essential oils can help release stress, anxiety, and depression.

PART 5:

HOW TO FOLLOW YOUR PATH IN THE RIGHT WAY

18.
Follow Your Goal

*"It's only when you make the process your
goal that the big dream can follow."*
Oprah Winfrey

Whatever you choose to do in your life, you need to ensure it is because you *want* to do it. If you have a dream and you want to follow it, make sure it is your dream. If you have a goal, make sure it is *your* goal – do not work to satisfy another person's dream. It is your life; you only have one, and time is ticking away. Every second counts, so why do something others want instead of what you want?

You have a purpose in your life. It can be to serve others, but it needs to be *your* purpose and not that of someone else. I know it is difficult and can be scary, but you do not have to risk it all. You have to walk before your run.

Therefore, if you want to do something – change your life, gain new experiences, and so on –think of the Power of One Second and start now by doing some research on what you want to do, and then follow the foundation process we discussed earlier. Start small, do your daily ritual, and you will become big. You need small wins to start – one second each time – and believe me, you will achieve your goal. As we have discussed, you need to harness your willpower to be able to make big jumps, but if you are not there yet, do not push yourself too much and start small.

If you want to start a new business, you do not have to quit your job. Do it in your spare time, but make sure you add it to your daily ritual. Once it grows, you can leave your current job and focus on your business. If you want to start to eat healthily, do not go for a one-month diet; do it for five days, eat what you want for two days, and then continue the next week with another five days, until you "act without thinking," and do it for extended periods of time. If you want to go out with someone, do not think you want to marry this person, think about going for a coffee and seeing how you both will feel.

You have a dream, a passion, and you can follow it without sacrificing everything. Follow the process we discussed and the growth in you will follow. I am insisting it be your goal because if it is yours, it means it is closer to your heart, and you will show the love that it deserves. If you show love, nothing can stop you, and nothing can take love away from you. It is yours forever, buried in you – success or failure – and it does not matter, as you have already changed, grown, and experienced new things that add meaning to your life and the lives of others.

19.
Have Balance

"Pan metron ariston" (Everything in moderation)
Greek Proverb

This proverb is very important, and even if it does not currently match your beliefs, when you start applying balance to your life, you will be able to see a great shift in the way you think, act, and live. I know that some people do not agree with this proverb because they are passionate and want to live their life to the extreme. However, **following your path in the right way is living a life that is sustainable.**

Sustainable does not mean boring; it just means you do not consume all of your energy all of the time – instead, you save energy as you go so that you can live and enjoy life longer. For example, if someone wants to live life to its full potential and sacrifices his sleep, then he will be sleep-deprived, which can cause depression, accidents, weight gain, and even death. Therefore, in order to follow the path the right way, you need to find balance in your actions.

Also, having a balance means you can experience a full day every day. Balance means that in your daily ritual, you should have activities that relate to your goals in all areas: financial/business, relationships, self-development, and health/fitness. In that way, every day is important, and you feel you have done something that will take you closer to your goal: you have exercised; so your body is strong and healthy; you have spent time with family and friends, which has made you feel connected and loved; you have worked on your business and work, and you were productive, and you have studied, and you have learned new things about life.

There is no need to sacrifice any of those things, so put them in your daily plan, and you will have time to do everything. Go back to Part 3 of this book if you struggle with time. I was struggling with time, but now waking up at 5:00 A.M. I have four hours in which to do everything I want to do before I go to work, and I am more productive – it is like having nine hours of extra time for me, and I still sleep seven hours a day. The earlier you wake up; the more time you will have to do the things you want.

You do not have to follow what I am doing, but as we discussed, you must reflect on what *you* are doing and adjust your actions accordingly. Try new things for one day or one week, and see how these actions impact the goals you want to achieve.

20.
Focus On Love

"Whatever the question, love is the answer."
Wayne Dyer

Whatever you do, whichever path you take, you need to learn to love yourself.

No one is perfect – you are the most beautiful, intelligent, loving person, and you do not need to be perfect. You do not need to be right, either. You are not a robot; you are an emotional human being. Reflect on what you might have done wrong, but never criticize, judge, or hurt yourself. Be respectful, be kind, and forgive yourself. If you have done something wrong, correct it and learn from it. If you are off-track with your goals, be aware of that, and get on track again.

You have very beautiful energy in you that is waiting to come out and show you the way. Much research has shown that self-love is key for mental health and well-being, as it fights depression and anxiety. You cannot achieve great things until you start loving yourself.

You also need to love others. You may have difficulty loving others because they may have said or done something to you, but you need to call your higher self and forgive. When you think bad things about others, it poisons your heart. The more you think about the wrongs, the more poison is thrown into your blood. The best solution is to forgive and forget – if these people are toxic, you can love them but remove them from your life.

Everyone is fighting their own battles, and some battles are easier than others. We never know why someone behaved in a certain way, which is why we need to forgive and love everyone.

Everyone needs to be forgiven because everyone can change and become a better person. Give them a good name so they will want to keep it.

Also, you will be more connected and caring if you love yourself and others. The more people you love and who love you back, the stronger the foundation and support you will have in your life. If something bad happens to you, or if you need some help or advice, you will be able to get it. This creates a feeling of safety and security, which can take some stress away from your life, so you can see things with clear eyes.

21.
Have Moral Excellence

*"I fully realize that no wealth or position can
long endure unless built upon truth and justice."*
Napoleon Hill

Moral excellence is vital for your long-term achievement. You might have reached your goal, but if you have achieved it in the wrong way, it will not be sustainable. Moral excellence needs to be embraced in your daily life. These are the things you consistently aspire to when no one is watching. I have selected three virtues that can guide you in achieving your goal:

Integrity: Know and do what is right; do not be afraid to speak for what you believe, keep your commitments, and be honest to yourself and others. This will take you a long way, as you will no longer have to hide. People can trust you, as you are reliable in what you believe and what you support.

Respect: Value everyone, regardless of their backgrounds and beliefs. Listen, be empathetic, and say thank you. Treat them with kindness, value, compassion, and appreciation. Start with respecting yourself, and others will follow. Being respectful means that the people you work with can become more motivated as they feel more valued. Also, as they build respect with others, they will start supporting each other and being more collaborative, which can increase productivity and morale. Just think that the person you speak to is the most important person in the world and the one you admire, and talk to him in the right way.

Philotimo: This is a Greek word that is impossible to translate because it describes a complex array of virtues. The etymology comes from *philos*, which means friend, and *timi*, which means honor. Therefore, it means you have honor. However, this translation is not even close to what *philotimo* means. I think the best way to describe *philotimo* is to describe its main ingredients, which are **integrity**, **respect**, **honor**, and **pride**. Integrity, because you have to do what is right and keep your commitments; respect because you need to value other people and not take advantage of them; honor, because you have to defend what you believe in; and pride, because your actions are based on helping others without wanting something in return.

A great example of *philotimo* occurred during World War II when a Nazi commander requested Bishop Chrysostomos and Mayor Loukas Karrer to give him the list of all names of Jews on the island of Zakynthos so they could be executed. Instead of giving the names, they helped the Jews hide in the mountains and returned the list to the commander with just two names – their own – saving hundreds of Jews.

Again, remember that you are not a robot and that you are human. Maybe it is challenging to have moral excellence all the time, perhaps you did not have moral excellence before, but now as you read this book, you want to change. We are all humans, and we all make mistakes. The important thing is to learn from those mistakes and use the knowledge to help you and those around you.

**It does not take more than one second
to change your life or the lives of others.**

Conclusion

You now know to use the Power of One Second and the Formula of Achievement to change and transform your life. Your transformation is a journey, which starts in one second and will continue as long as you do the work with intention. We have shown you that everything is possible, and if you find the actions that will help you achieve your goal and follow your path in the right way, not only will it help you, but it will also help the people around you, and together we will make this world a better place.

I have tried to show you how to do this by using my personal experience, the experiences of others, neuroscience, and ancient Chinese and Indian techniques. I have used these resources to convince you and provide evidence to you that it is possible.

I believe that everyone has some knowledge about what they need to do to achieve what they want if they raise their consciousness and awareness.

I have given you techniques that you can practice to help you achieve your goals, but what is more important is that you try them and see what works for you. If something does not work for you, find your own way, create your own practices, or enhance and tweak the existing ones and see what impact those actions have in your life and if they take you closer to your goal. Share them with this community through mindbodism.com, and let's together make this world a better place.

There are a lot of topics covered in this book, and some concepts can only be understood and practiced by reading the chapters of the book again and again. Try to have this book somewhere where you can see it daily, such as in front of your desk, so that it can act as a reminder that you can use the Power of One Second and that you have the power to achieve anything you want in your life. If you cannot start, if you have started but you have stopped, if you want to keep going, if you are still trying to find your path, if you do not know how to follow your path in the right way, just read the book again.

Also, inspired by this book, I have created mindbodism.com, so you can find techniques, practices, and courses for your mind, body, and spirit that will create balance and meaning in your life. Also, because of my samadhi experience and awakening, I will publish my second book, *My Spiritual Reality*, in November 2023 in which I will share with you my personal spiritual experience and provide evidence that Albert Einstein was right when he said, "There are two ways to live your life. One is as though nothing is a miracle. The other is as though everything is a miracle."

Made in United States
Orlando, FL
10 January 2024

42343646R00100